WESKER

D1629964

THEIR VERY OWN AND GOLDEN CITY

... and accordingly the Trade Unionists and their leaders who were once the butt of the most virulent abuse from the whole of the Upper and Middle classes are now praised and petted by them because they do tacitly or openly acknowledge the necessity for the master's existence; it is felt that they are no longer the enemy; the class struggle in England is entering into a new phase, which may even make the once dreaded Trade Unions allies of capital, since they in their turn form a kind of privileged group among the workmen; in fact they now no longer represent the whole class of workers as working *men* but rather as charged with the office of keeping the human part of the capitalists' machinery in good working order and freeing it from any grit of discontent...

Now that's the blind alley which the Trade Unions have now got into; I say again if they are determined to have masters to manage their affairs, they must expect in turn to pay for that luxury ... remembering that the price they pay for their so-called captains of industry is no mere money payment – no mere tribute which once paid leaves them free to do as they please, but an authoritative ordering of the whole tenor of their lives, what they shall eat, drink, wear, what houses they shall have, books, or newspapers rather, they shall read, down to the very days on which they shall take their holidays like a drove of cattle driven out from the stable to grass.

WILLIAM MORRIS: *from a lecture on 'Socialism' given at the Victoria Hall, Norwich, on March 8th, 1886*

THEIR VERY OWN
AND
GOLDEN CITY

*A play in Two Acts
and twenty-nine Scenes*

by

ARNOLD WESKER

JONATHAN CAPE
THIRTY BEDFORD SQUARE
LONDON

PRINTED IN GREAT BRITAIN BY
LATIMER TREND & CO. LTD., PLYMOUTH
ON PAPER MADE BY JOHN DICKINSON & CO. LTD.
BOUND BY A. W. BAIN & CO. LTD., LONDON

First presentation of the play was at the Royal Court Theatre, London, in the summer of 1966, with the following cast:

Andrew Cobham	IAN MCKELLEN
Jessie Sutherland	GILLIAN MARTELL
John Casper	GEORGE HOWE
Jake Latham	SEBASTIAN SHAW
Smithy	BERNARD GALLAGHER
Kate Ramsay	ANN FIRBANK
Priest	ROGER BOOTH
Stoney Jackson	WILLIAM STEWART
Paul Dobson	JOHN SHEPHERD
Chairman of Local Town Planning Committee	RICHARD BUTLER
Officer of Ministry of Town and Country Planning	
	SEBASTIAN SHAW
Ted Worthington	BERNARD GALLAGHER
Bill Matheson	RICHARD BUTLER
Brian Cambridge	JOSEPH GREIG
Toastmaster	ROGER BOOTH
Maisy	JANNETTE LEGGE
Guests, etc.	DAVID LELAND
	JAQUELINE HARRISON
	JANET CHAPPELL
	JANNETTE LEGGE
	KENNETH CRANHAM

To my dear friend Tom Maschler

LIST OF CHARACTERS

ACT I ANDREW COBHAM ⎫
       JESSIE SUTHERLAND ⎬ *as youngsters*
       PAUL DOBSON ⎭
       STONEY JACKSON
       ANDREW COBHAM, *an architect*
       JESSIE SUTHERLAND, *his wife*
       PAUL DOBSON, *a journalist*
       STONEY JACKSON, *a minister*
       JAKE LATHAM, *an old trade union organizer*
       SMITHY, *a local Labour Party chairman*
       KATE RAMSEY, *a daughter of local aristocracy*, JAKE'*s friend*
       JOHN CASPER, *an architect*, ANDREW'*s employer*

ACT II CHAIRMAN OF LOCAL TOWN PLANNING COMMITTEE
        OFFICER OF MINISTRY OF TOWN & COUNTRY PLANNING
        ALFIE HARRINGTON, *an industrialist*
        REGINALD MAITLAND, *Minister of Town & Country Planning*
        TED WORTHINGTON ⎫
        BILL MATHESON ⎬ *trade union leaders*
        BRIAN CAMBRIDGE ⎭
        TOASTMASTER

Couples for crowd scenes from whom can be taken three walk-ons
and possibly some of the above-mentioned minor characters.

NOTE

Because of the construction of this play – which is in the form of a
'flash-forward' (as opposed to 'flash-back') – two sets of actors may
be needed to play ANDREW COBHAM, JESSICA SUTHERLAND, PAUL

DOBSON, STONEY JACKSON: one set of young actors to whom we constantly return in the setting of the Cathedral, and another set who will act out the play from being young men and women to old ones. But in the London version one set of actors played both parts and this established a particular style to the production. Both approaches could work. (See note at end of play.)

The following characters can be played by the same actor:
JAKE LATHAM *and* REGINALD MAITLAND
WORTHINGTON *and* SMITHY
JOHN CASPER *and* ALFIE HARRINGTON
CHAIRMAN *and* MATHESON

SCENES:

SCENES

Andy's study

Durham Cathedral

N.B. If the cathedral scenes in either Act are heavily
played this entire play will fail. Innocence, gaiety
and a touch of lunacy is their atmosphere.

The author is aware that certain instances in the play do not
conform to actual Trade Union or Labour Party procedure, and
hopes that the poetic licence he has taken will be understood.

ACT ONE

Scene 1

Empty stage.
A young man enters, ANDREW COBHAM. *He carries a drawing-board and a knapsack.*
What he is looking at he is seeing for the first time. It is the year 1926.
Fade in back projection of interior of Durham Cathedral.
Sound of Bach on an organ. Magic, discovery.

ANDY (*with surprise*). I – am as big as – it. They built cathedrals for one man – it's just big enough. (*He closes his eyes.*) Show me love and I'll hate no one. Give me wings and I'll build you a city. Teach me to fly and I'll do beautiful deeds. (*He opens his eyes and looks up at the roof, turning round in wonderment at the same time.*) Hey God, do you hear that? Beautiful deeds, I said.

(JESSICA SUTHERLAND *wanders in.*)

JESSIE. Andy?

ANDY. For one man, Jessie, a cathedral is built for one man.

JESSIE. Do you talk to yourself?

ANDY. Every man should have a cathedral in his back garden.

JESSIE. I've never heard you talk to yourself.

ANDY. Look at the way that roof soars.

JESSIE. Talk to yourself and you'll go mad.

ANDY. Doesn't it make you love yourself?

JESSIE. 'Those whom the gods wish to destroy they first turn mad.'

ANDY. When a man loves himself he loves the world. Listen.
        (*Music swells.*)
    I reckon the gods touch composers with a fever every night. I bet Bach got to heaven before Shakespeare. Look.

(*Sunlight strikes through the coloured glass.*)

Jessie, if you'll marry me I'll build you a house that soars – like this cathedral. And you, you'll give me six beautiful children, and they'll soar, mad, like that roof there. How's that?

JESSIE. The gods'll destroy you, that's for sure.

ANDY. Today, Jessie, I know, I know. I know everything I want to do with my life.

(*Wanders around in a trance.*

The youngsters PAUL DOBSON, STONEY JACKSON *wander in. They too have been affected by the cathedral's interior.*)

JESSIE. I found him talking to himself.

STONEY. And God no doubt.

PAUL. It's that roof. The audacity, the cheek, to build like this.

STONEY. Blessed. They were blessed.

PAUL. Blessed? The men who built this? Never! Blasphemous, more like. To try to reach your God with pillars like these – blasphemous. Bless 'em.

ANDY. Supposing you had the chance to build a city, a new one, all the money in the world, supposing that; this new city – what would you do with it?

STONEY. He's off.

ANDY. What would you chuck out, have done with?

PAUL. Just look at it, man. Don't question, look.

ANDY. The chance to change the pattern of living for all time? There it is, all virgin, new land, lovely, green, rich, what would we do with it? Supposing that? What would us do?

STONEY. I wouldn't. I wouldn't even bother to answer 'cos I'd know the money would never be there.

JESSIE. But if it were?

STONEY. Trust you to encourage him.

PAUL. Why not? Supposing. All these people, pooling their money, for a city, just supposing.

STONEY. You suppose, I can't.

14

JESSIE. Well, what would us do?

STONEY. You don't expect answers, do you?

ANDY. Did you know people thought the invention of the printing press was just a new technique for producing books?

STONEY. He's off again.

JESSIE. Wasn't it?

ANDY. Was it, hell! 'Is that you up there, God?' we yelled. And presto! A thousand books came out. 'No,' they said.

STONEY. Andy!

ANDY. 'No.' Presto like that.

JESSIE. But everyone knows it.

ANDY. They don't, they don't. Aye, they know they can read a book on any subject under the sun, that they know. But it's more, the printing press meant more. It meant something could be done which a long time ago couldn't be done, change! That's what the printing press meant – change.

STONEY. Change! Change! You always want to be changing things.

ANDY. No! I just want to know, all the time, that change is possible. Then, when it's needed, I'll do it. STAND CLEAR.

(ANDY *stands on his head.*)

JESSIE. Get up, you idiot, someone'll see you.

ANDY (*still on his head*). Stoney, you're sulkin'. (*Returns to crouching position.*) Don't sulk, Stoney. A thousand books said 'no', honest they did.

STONEY. And another thousand said 'yes'.

ANDY. Stoney, I love you, I don't have to love God also, do I? Kiss me. (*No response.*) I'll kiss you then. (*Gives STONEY a long kiss then immediately stands on his head again.*) You know, it's almost as impressive this end up.

JESSIE. You ragged-arsed apprentice, this cathedral's done things to you.

ANDY. Perhaps they should build them upside down.

JESSIE. Get back, I tell you, they'll throw us out. Paul, Stoney – do something, tell him.

STONEY. Leave him, he looks prettier.

ANDY (*descending to crouching position again*). And when I'm older I'll meet someone who's educated, and he'll look at me 'cos I've got an interesting face and we'll talk together and he'll think – 'this lad's not like the others, I think I can do something with him' – and we'll have long discussions – STAND CLEAR. (*Returns to standing on his head.*)

JESSIE. Get off your head, Andy, stand on your feet.

PAUL. You won't control him.

JESSIE. Andy!

(PAUL *and* STONEY *wander off to start their sketching.*)

ANDY. I'll meet all sorts of people, learn all sorts of things – I'll have good friends, Jessie Sutherland, good people, all of them. (*Returns to his feet.*)

JESSIE. That's better. I wonder you've any blood left in your feet. Now what are you doing? Why are you limping?

(ANDY *moves to unwrap his board and pencils.*)

ANDY. Broke me leg down a mine.

JESSIE. You've never been down a mine.

ANDY. Look at that mad roof, Jessie – that's the height a man is, a house should be built that high. (*Starts to draw.*)

JESSIE. Does Mr Casper know that you're studying architecture out of office hours?

ANDY. He knows.

JESSIE. Isn't he impressed?

ANDY. Why should he be, he doesn't believe I'll succeed.

JESSIE. Will you though?

ANDY. I should be in college, studying, full time.

JESSIE. Succeed – will you?

ANDY. But what's a poor lad to do without cash?

JESSIE. I'm asking you, will you though?

ANDY. Instead, I am suffering.

JESSIE. Thee? Suffer? Tha'll never suffer, tha's too cheeky.

ANDY. Aye, I'll succeed. I'll end up architecting. You know it in a place like this.

JESSIE. How sure you sound.

ANDY. Old Casper will totter around mumbling to himself, 'You're a draughtsman, a good draughtsman, good draughtsmen can't be found every day, be satisfied, the good Lord made you a draughtsman don't argue with him.' And then the news will come through that I've passed and he'll go on mumbling, 'brilliant, clever boy, the good Lord's made you an architect, praise Him then, mumble, mumble, mumble.' And he'll offer me a partnership, you'll see – dear God, look how that ceiling soars.

Scene 2

It is the year 1933.

Architect's Office.

JOHN CASPER, *head of the firm, is in his office with* ANDY.

CASPER *is unfolding over a blackboard some of his favourite designs.*

CASPER. This is the Williamson design for a church. Splendid architect, Williamson, a great architect. The good Lord made a great architect to design that church – Williamson.

ANDY. It doesn't soar though, does it?

CASPER. Soar! Soar! Every building doesn't have to soar, Mr Cobham. I sometimes think you must suffer from megalomania.

ANDY. Don't stop, Mr Casper.

CASPER. I must be quite mad doing this for you, Cobham. I'm sure the normal routine of this office would have taken your mind off your results as well. It's most irresponsible of me to encourage you in this wish to be an architect. You're a draughtsman, a good draughtsman, be satisfied that the good Lord – with my help – made you a draughtsman.

ANDY. Jessie promised to ring through, Mr Casper. I've never asked you to do this before – it'll be soon.

CASPER. Besides, I'm sure you've gathered my tastes after five years working with me.

ANDY. Just occupy me a little longer.

CASPER. This is perhaps my favourite – John Martin's almshouses for the old people in Cirencester. Lovely houses, beautiful square – look at those gardens –

ANDY. Was it the good Lord made those or John Martin?

CASPER. Now you mock me, Cobham.

ANDY. Nay, I'm jesting, tha's a gentle man, I'd never mock thee.
    (*The phone rings.*)

CASPER. Thank God, now perhaps I can get my work done.

ANDY (*lifts phone, listens, is stunned*). Thank you. (*Pause.*) Yes – I can hear you. (*Replaces receiver. Silence.*)

CASPER. You haven't passed. You *have* passed? They've accepted your designs? Andy lad? Look at him, has the good Lord struck you dumb? You've passed?
    (ANDY *can only smile.*)
You have passed then. Well then, well I never then. The good Lord *has* made you an architect – well then. It says a lot about me, doesn't it, lad? I must see those designs again, where are they, those 'testimonies of study'? (*Looks.*) These them? (*Unfolds plans.*) Soar? Soar? Is this what you mean by soar? Yes, well it says a lot about me then.
    (CASPER *lays down plans, walks once round the still silent* ANDREW, *then faces him, stretches out his arms and embraces him.*)
You must register with the Council of Architects, you

must qualify, straight away you must do it, now to begin with, at once and then, Andrew, I'll make an offer – listen to me, talking of offers so soon, it's indecent – never mind, I'm delighted, delighted. Chief Assistant, share of the profits and promise of a partnership in two years if all goes well. What do you say? I'll ring up my solicitors now, this minute, draw up a contract, are you listening? Do you hear me? Cobham! Andrew! What are you doing? The blood'll run to your head, Andrew –

(*While* ANDY *stands on his head the scene changes to –*)

Scene 3

A riverside, some hours later.
ANDY *still on his head.*
JESSIE *unpacking a picnic.*
ANDY. 'I'll ring up my solicitors, now, this minute,' he said, 'draw up a contract, share of the profits, a partnership –'
JESSIE. Andy Cobham, stand on your feet, you're a big lad now. What did you say?
ANDY (*returning to his feet*). Casper's a good man, a gentle man, but he's a dull architect. I'll not stay with him.
JESSIE. Whose practice will you join then?
ANDY. I shan't join a practice. I'll join the local Council, gain more experience.
JESSIE. What do they pay?
ANDY. Pay?
JESSIE. Are we to live on nothing when we marry?
ANDY. Oh aye – marry.
JESSIE. Look how your moods change. What is it now, Andy? (*Silence.*) Andy, I'm asking you. Sometimes I have to squeeze words from you – Andy.

ANDY. Can you feel the sun on you, Jessie? Take off your blouse.

JESSIE. Don't be mad – on a common field – to take off – undress – don't be mad.

ANDY. It's all happened with too much ease, Jessie, not much struggle.

JESSIE. Not much struggle? You! You lap up action like a kitten with milk – you wouldn't know you'd struggled till you died.

ANDY. The year of depression for everyone else but the world's going right for me.

JESSIE. Depression! Hitler! All my father does is talk of depressions and wars near by and round corners and on horizons.

ANDY. Your father's not a fool, then, he's heard the news. Terrible news, all over Europe, Jessie. Hard to believe with the sun on your back.

JESSIE. Will there be bombs, then, and killing, and destruction?

ANDY. Destruction? Aye, the cities will fall.

JESSIE. You frighten me, Andy.

ANDY. I want six children from you, Jessie. One after another, six of them.

JESSIE. Mind me, Andy, you're hurting me – Andy!

ANDY. Andy, Andy, chocolate pandy, that's what my kids will say, with buttons and beans and cabbage greens and rainbows every day. Jessie, it's very cold being young, isn't it, lass?

(*Suddenly* ANDY *hoists her over his shoulder.*)

Give me twelve children, twenty children –

JESSIE. Put me down, you bullying oaf, put me down, I'm feeling sick. Put me down or there'll be no children, you're pushing my belly in –

ANDY (*jumping*). – and in and in and in and in. (*Changes her*

20

position into his arms.) Who wants a girl more complicated than you? You're simple like a cottage loaf and pure-smelling like a rose.

JESSIE. Simple! Simple! Cottage loaves and apple dumplings! You don't think me foolish by any chance? I mean I'd not be happy knowing we were married just 'cos we've been together these years. You wouldn't marry anyone you thought a fool – you wouldn't, would you, would you, Andy?

ANDY. Do you love me?

JESSIE. I love you.

ANDY. How do you know?

JESSIE. Because I love myself.

ANDY. That's a terrible conceit.

JESSIE. Conceit? But you taught me. Love yourself and you love the world. Well, I'm full of myself. I feel beautiful. Every bit of me. Look. Isn't every bit of me the most beautiful thing you've ever seen? Cottage loaves and dumplings and roses and all?

(*He releases her.*)

Now look, you've changed again. You see, you change from mood to mood at such a speed.

ANDY. It's just – I'm thinking that near by it sounds like such a dreadful war that all I want to do is eat the cottage loaf and smell the rose. You've a lovely face, Jessie, lovely, lovely, lovely.

JESSIE. Catch me then.

(JESSIE *picks up picnic satchel and runs.*)

(*Off.*) Catch me, catch me. (*Silence.*) I've found another spot – the ground is softer – Andeeeeeee catch meeeeee.

(ANDY *remains as scene slowly changes to* –)

ACT ONE

Scene 4

Some months later.

A public house.

A group of eight people including JAKE LATHAM, SMITHY, ANDREW COBHAM, *have gathered after a trade union branch meeting.*

SMITHY. To our retiring chairman, a toast. Jake Latham.

    (All raise glasses.)

JAKE. My last term as chairman and only eight members turned up. Even my resolution was defeated. Pathetic, isn't it? Three officials, five members and one of them is new – and our books show a membership of 259.

SMITHY. Bloody trade union branch meeting? Funeral parlour more like – where no one liked the dead 'un.

JAKE. Ninteen thirty-three will go down as one of the blackest years – I'll never understand.

SMITHY. Well you was daft to try passing a resolution on education with only a few of us here. And besides, you can't ask us to support the spending of money on education when there's no houses.

JAKE. I'm too old for your slogans about empty stomachs, Smithy, what about empty heads? Look at us. We might just as well have had the whole branch meeting in the pub.

SMITHY. Give us a farewell speech, Jake. Say something.

JAKE. Goodbye.

SMITHY. Don't be mean.

JAKE. You mean I've got to return something for that dreary old medal of service? All right, I'll ask a question then. I know it's answers the young always want but I'm afraid this old 'un's going to be different – that's my reputation anyway, being different, a stale sort of reputation I'm feeling now. I haven't got answers so let's bequeath them a question eh, young Cobham? What holds a movement together? Any movement, not even a movement, a group of people, say, or a family, or a nation or a civilization? Something must. And *we* didn't find it, God help us, *we* didn't find it.

It's a lousy year, 1933, I don't like it at all, a miserable year in which to end office. Gentlemen, here's to you.

(JAKE *breaks away to buy another drink.* ANDY *follows him.*)

If you want apologies for my morbidity you won't get it.

ANDY. I'm not afraid of a challenge.

JAKE. Challenge, is it? An optimist, are you?

ANDY. An optimist? Yes brother, I suppose I am.

JAKE. Brother! Well, I mayn't ever have the opportunity to temper your optimism but I can advise you to drop the jargon. Brother! A useless title, full of empty love.

ANDY. A traditional greeting, Mr Latham; it's got a good history.

JAKE. Use history, don't imitate it. Brother! Let's face facts! Let us stand together! It's only with strong determination that we can go forward! Jargon.

ANDY. If the old words are failing us then perhaps they'd better be rescued, not abandoned.

JAKE. Don't confuse breathing new life with the perpetuation of stale breath.

ANDY. You prefer homely maxims to jargon, is it?

JAKE. That was not a homely maxim and don't be cheeky.

ANDY. Don't be – ?

JAKE. – cheeky. I'm a clever man, Mr Cobham, but I'm an old and vain one. I could teach you a lot but I can't bear a young 'un who doesn't know his place.

ANDY. Know his – ?

JAKE. – place. Stop gawping – you'll get lockjaw. I've no time for rebels, they hate the past for what it didn't give them. The Labour Movement is choked with bad-mannered, arrogant little rebels who enjoy kicking stubborn parents in the teeth. Revolutionaries is what we want –

23

they spend less time rebelling against what's past and give their energy to the vision ahead.

ANDY. 'The vision ahead'? I thought that was the jargon we should drop, Mr Latham.

JAKE. Oh ye gods! Good night, Mr Cobham. (*Makes to go.*)

ANDY. Jake Latham!

(JAKE *stops.*)

What could you teach me?

Scene 5

As ANDY *and* JAKE *look at each other the scene changes to* JAKE's *study, some weeks later.*

JAKE. When you come to me and say 'teach me' what do you mean? No, first – why me?

ANDY. I've always had a picture in my mind of an old, sorry –

JAKE. Yes, yes, old, I'm old, don't fumble, I'm old.

ANDY. A man, somebody, who'd talk to me. Don't misunderstand me, I don't want to be told what to think. I've read, I've always read, but I've never been, well, guided. Waste, I can't bear waste. I may die young, you see.

JAKE. Huh! romantic as well. An optimistic romantic! I'd say you were doomed, Cobham. Go home.

ANDY. I'm not impressed with cynicism, Mr Latham, it's a bit dull is cynicism. You say I'm damned and it sounds clever I know, but I'm not impressed. Neither were you, were you?

JAKE. Are you patronizing me, young lad, are you?

ANDY. Mr Latham, I –

JAKE. I've been chairman of my branch, Cobham, on and off for the last twenty years, chairman of a local trade union branch in a dreadful and dreary industrial town. Does it occur to you to ask why someone like me is a chairman only of a local branch – does it?

ANDY. Perhaps you'll tell me in good time but just now –

JAKE. Right! Learn? You want to learn? Answer me this then, Ramsay MacDonald handed in his resignation as Labour Prime Minister two years ago and assumed the Leadership of a National Coalition Government. What led up to that 1931 crisis?

ANDY. I work in an architect's office, Mr Latham, I want to build cities, I'm not a student of economics.

JAKE. How interesting. You want to build cities but you don't want to know about economics.

ANDY. Do I have to know about economics before I'm permitted to build my cities?

JAKE. Your cities, eh?

ANDY. Why laugh at me? Is it every day someone comes to you and says 'teach me'?

JAKE. No. Never, actually. No one's ever given me such a responsibility. Laugh, do I? Daft old man, me. I'm a bit overwhelmed perhaps. I don't know what to teach you, lad. It must have been the vanity of an old man made me invite you here. I'm not a teacher. I've got a pocket full of principles, that's all really. If you'd tried to answer my question I'd have tried to apply those principles, but … There *was* a principle involved in that crisis you know. It wasn't very widely argued but it was there. Do you know what the Bank of England did – poor bloody Ramsay Macdonald – they frightened the pants off him. All our gold was going, you see, flowing out of the window it was, people drawing left, right and centre. So the directors of the Bank demanded to see the Prime Minister and give him their view of the situation. And what was their view? They said to him: 'MacDonald, old son, this isn't a financial problem, it's a political one. No one abroad will lend

25

us any money because they are worried about your government,' they said. 'The Labour Government is squandering', they said, 'too much money on silly things, frivolous things, social services and education,' they said. 'Foreigners don't trust your government, Mr MacDonald, they don't think you can handle the affairs of the British nation.' Huh! You wouldn't think that a Labour Prime Minister would fall for anything as simple as that, would you? But he did, old MacDonald. 'You're right,' he said to the Bank of England. 'We *have* been silly, I'll make cuts.' So he tried, but he didn't have all the Cabinet with him, and he resigned, formed a coalition government and then made the cuts. It's almost unbelievable, isn't it? Where does the principle come in? I'll tell you. Would it have been unreasonable to expect a socialist government to apply socialist economic principles instead of the usual patchwork? It wouldn't, would it? But did they? (*Mocking.*) 'The time isn't ripe! The government'll be defeated!' The sort of answer we all give when we don't do the things we feel are right. So here's the question: is it better to risk defeat in defence of a principle or hang on with compromises?

ANDY. Do you want me to answer?

JAKE. Of course not, just listen. People always need to know that someone was around who acted. Defeat doesn't matter; in the long run all defeat is temporary. It doesn't matter about present generations but future ones always want to look back and know that someone was around acting on principle. That government, I tell you, should've screamed out to the opposition 'REVOLUTION' – like that. 'Control imports! Clamp down on speculators! Revolution!' Like that, at the top of its voice; and then, taken hold of British industry by the scruff of its neck and made it develop, themselves, full employment! And per-

haps they'd have crashed – it was a doomed government anyway – and perhaps we'd have shuddered. But after the crash, after the shuddering and the self-pitying and the recriminations, we'd have been stunned with admiration and the sounds of the crash would've echoed like bloody great hallelujahs, bloody great hallelujahs –
What the hell you standing on your head for? You silly or something? Apoplectic?

ANDY. It's relaxing, I'm happy.

JAKE. You're a vegetarian also, I suppose?

ANDY. Here, you try it.

JAKE. Me?

ANDY. I'll make it easy for you. (*Lies on his back and raises his knees.*) Put your hands on my knees.

JAKE. Certainly not.

ANDY. You're so dull, you politicians. I'll catch you.

(KATHERINE RAMSAY *enters.*)

KATE. How amusing, Jake.

JAKE. Andrew Cobham, this is Katherine Ramsay; Kate – Andrew Cobham.

ANDY. Evening. I didn't know you were expecting a visitor.

JAKE. Sit down, boy, I've invited her so that you two could meet. Kate is the daughter of Lord and Lady Ramsay – the local landlords. Her mother and I were once er – we were – we, were in love.

KATE. You can almost see him stiffen, Jake – I thought you said he was different.

JAKE. Beautiful woman – Kate's mum – rare, strong. Great scandal! And my puritanical colleagues never let me forget it. Thank God I'm also a good organizer.

KATE. You're a draughtsman, Mr –

ANDY. Cobham's the name.

(ANDY *attempts to leave.*)

JAKE. What you rushing for?

ANDY. My fiancée – I'm meeting her.

KATE. Why do you limp, Mr – ?

ANDY. Cobham's the name.

JAKE. Why does he what?

ANDY. I used to be a miner, Miss, and one day the props gave way and I used my leg instead – for five hours till help came. I've not been able to use it since.

KATE. But you –

ANDY. Good night, then, glad to have met you, Miss – er – Kate.

KATE. Kate!

ANDY. Thank you, Jake.

(ANDY *goes, limping badly and bravely.*)

JAKE. Mine? He's never been near a mine.

KATE. Of course not, Jake, he's never been near a mine.

Scene 6

ANDY's *bedsitter, some days later.* KATE *enters.*

KATE. Why did you run away from Jake's that night?

ANDY. You're a forward lass, coming upon me like this.

KATE. Were you afraid?

ANDY. How did you know I'd be in?

KATE. It's my nature to take chances. Were you afraid?

ANDY. I bet you smoke pipes.

KATE. No, cigars. Were you afraid?

ANDY. I try not to be feared of anything.

KATE. Why did you go so quickly then?

ANDY. How you do persist.

KATE. Persistence is a family trait. You turned on your heel because my mother is Lady Ramsay, didn't you? I want you to know, Mr Cobham, I'm a classless woman.

28

ANDY. Aye, I can see it.

KATE. I can't bear people who wear their class on their hearts like an emblem.

ANDY. Seems to me you're more intent in denying it than I am in looking for it.

KATE. I want us to be friends.

ANDY. You sound desperate.

KATE. Passionate, not desperate. You must know certain things about me, Mr Cobham.

ANDY. I don't see as I must know anything. I was brought up to earn friendship.

KATE. That's our difference then, I don't have to earn anything, I was born with rights.

ANDY. Aye, of course, you're a classless woman.

KATE. You're a fool if you think I'm talking about class rights. Human rights, Mr Cobham, from any class. There are certain people who are born with natures that naturally deserve love and respect. Yours, like mine, is one of them.

ANDY. I think you're seeing me as you want.

KATE. Oh? You really see yourself as a humble man? You shame yourself with false modesty?

ANDY. I don't see as how modesty is always false, and I don't see as how being capable and ambitious should make me immodest. I am what I am, I don't feel the need to boast it loudly or deny it. What I do is my boast, not what I say or don't say.

KATE. Charming, Andy, it becomes you.

ANDY. And I'm not needing your comments.

KATE. Don't be ungracious.

ANDY. I'm annoyed.

KATE. Don't be annoyed either, it's my nature to be direct.

ANDY. It's your nature to be a lot of things, it seems. Do you always talk about yourself?

KATE. I want us to be friends.

ANDY. You want, you want! You'll have to earn, young lady.

KATE. How long have you lived here?

ANDY. Eighteen months.

KATE (*referring to a chair*). Did you buy that monstrosity or does it belong here?

ANDY. It belongs here.

KATE. Why don't you get rid of it?

ANDY. It belongs here.

KATE. My dear, the landlady should be given to understand that you are doing her a kindness by getting rid of it.

ANDY. It's not my habit to interfere with other people's property.

KATE. And you're the socialist, are you? Look at this room. You want to be an architect? You want to build beautiful homes? Then how can you surround yourself with ugliness? Look how you dress, look what you hang on your walls. How can you dare plan other people's houses when you live with such mediocrity?

ANDY. I –

KATE. How can you dare?

ANDY. I – blast you, woman, I'll not have anyone talk at me like this.

KATE. Honesty hurts you, then?

ANDY. It's your tone of voice, it gets in the way.

KATE. Do you deny that I'm right?

ANDY. I'll not be dragged –

KATE. You deny I'm right?

ANDY. I'll not –

KATE. Do you?

ANDY. I'm attached to my surroundings. Personal things count for me. That' a truth also – attachments count.

KATE. Even attachments to the third-rate?

ANDY. You know, I'd agree with you if only that sneer in your voice didn't contradict the sense of your words. I don't like people who sneer.

KATE. Tell me, have you ever really worked down a mine?

ANDY. No.

KATE. Why did you limp, then?

ANDY. It's a joke I have.

KATE. Why look, you're blushing.

ANDY. Ye gods, has ever a person so twisted me all ways in so
short a time?

KATE. What is the joke?

ANDY. It's a silly joke.

KATE. Tell it me.

Scene 7

The Cathedral.

They are all sitting eating sandwiches.

STONEY. How will we really all end, I wonder? Will we stay
the friends we are?

ANDY. I remember at school we used to ask, 'Where shall us
be in five years from now – just five years?'

PAUL. Five years older.

STONEY. I've tomato sandwiches – who likes tomato sandwiches?

JESSIE. I'll swop half a pork pie for two of them.

STONEY. Don't like pork pies – they're all fat.

JESSIE. I made it myself.

(PAUL *starts coughing.*)

ANDY. Shut up coughing, Paul, and read us one of your
poems.

STONEY. Why do all poets die of consumption?

JESSIE. Give over, Stoney – the air here is none too good for a
cough like that.

STONEY. She doesn't speak much, but when she does – what
wisdom.

JESSIE. The gift for gabbing belongs to you, it's you who's
taking up religion.

ANDY. Stoney Jackson will be the most irreverent priest I
know.

PAUL.   You love me now but wait until
          Upon my lips you feed no more
          And in my arms you lie and scatter
          Lovely dreams you struggled for.
          Upon my heart you'll lay your head
          And know of things that matter more.

          So hard is love and soft its sighs
          And soft the contours of our lives,
          Not all your woman's winter tears
          Shall take you back among sweet sighs.
          You love me now but wait until
          You've crossed my love between your thighs.

          (*There is a long silence.*)

JESSIE. You were a gang when I first met you all.

ANDY. There's something about people getting together and
doing things.

JESSIE. You were all in Woolworth's together.

ANDY. I don't see the point of insisting you're an individual –
you're born one anyway.

JESSIE. I was fascinated.

ANDY. But a group together, depending on each other,
knowing what they want, knowing how to get it –

JESSIE. Stoney used pretend he was blind, and I remember
Paul could walk from one end of the city to the other
without looking up from his book.

ANDY. But a group together –

JESSIE. I watched you all –

ANDY. Now that's something.

JESSIE. You were pinching sweets.

STONEY. Ssh!

PAUL. What is it?

STONEY. They've started a service.

    (*Sound of choir,*
    ANDREW *mounts a tomb.*)

ANDY. I'll give a sermon.

JESSIE. Now they'll chuck us out, now sure as sure they'll chuck us out.

    (PAUL *and* STONEY *start applauding.*)

ANDY. Shut up, you ignorant proles you, don't you know you mustn't applaud in churches? Now, dearly beloved apprentices, my ragged-arsed brothers, my sermon today comes from the Bible.

STONEY. All sermons come from the Bible.

ANDY. Well, my Bible then. And the prophet Blake said, 'Bring me my bow of burning gold, bring me my arrows of desire.'

STONEY. Since when did you read Blake in the Bible?

ANDY. I didn't, I read the Bible in Blake – now hush! 'Bring me my spear, O clouds unfold, bring me my chariot of fire! I will not cease from mental strife, nor shall my sword sleep in my hand, till we have built Jerusalem in England's green and pleasant land.' Till we have built Jerusalem, dearly beloved apprentices, in England's green and pleasant land. Now, how can we build Jerusalem in England's green and pleasant land?

ALL. Get rid of the rotten houses!

ANDY. Right. Who built the rotten houses?

ALL. The property owners!

ANDY. Right. Who's going to kick the property owners out?

ALL. Labour!

ANDY. Right. Who's going to control the next government?

ALL. Labour!

ANDY. Right. And –

JESSIE. Quick, there's someone coming.

(ANDY *scampers down and everyone innocently turns to his sketching board. A* FROCKED PRIEST *walks through, smiling encouragingly at them.* ANDY *resumes his sermon, but not from the tomb.*)

ANDY. And when the new Labour comes, who will they turn to to build their homes?

ALL. Us!

ANDY. 'Boys', they'll say, no, 'Sons' – 'sons', that's what they'll call us. 'Our sons,' they'll say. 'We've done it, we won, now – to work, you ragged-arsed brothers. Build us homes.' That's what they'll say – 'Build us homes' – am I right, boys?

ALL. You're right –

Of course he's right –

Isn't he right –

He's always right –

Ssh!

(*They jubilantly run off to different parts to continue their sketching.*)

Scene 8

The riverside. It is the year 1935.

KATE *is waiting for* ANDY *who approaches.*

ANDY. New Labour! New Labour! We never learn, never!

KATE. I take it you're having housing problems with the local council.

ANDY. Patchwork, patchwork. It's like Jake says – they do nothing but patchwork.

KATE. What do you expect from clerks and butchers?

ANDY. Beware, beware, my brethren, of the woman who claims to be classless.

KATE. There's not even a dignified pause and 'bang' – look at your emancipated working class, leaping to adopt the values of simpering shopkeepers.

ANDY. She sneers, my God, how she sneers.

KATE. Stop fighting me, Andrew Cobham, my attacks are reserved for the half-hearted and insensitive. I don't attack a class, only certain kinds of human beings. Just because the bloody town council sits on your designs. You don't like the town council? Change them! Or join them –

(Pause.)

Ah! Join them! Now that's an idea. Tick tick tick tick. Look at that brain turning over and over.

ANDY. When a person talks, I think.

KATE. Tick tick tick tick. When Jake first introduced us I said, 'Keep an eye on that young man.'

ANDY. She's talking about herself again.

KATE. Tick tick tick tick. He will play his life like a game of chess, Jake, I said. Working ten moves ahead – a politician's way, really. But I suppose one will admire him, I said, for being a gambler – because if the first move is wrong he's gambled away the next nine.

ANDY. How clever the young Ramsay girl is, so observant about people, so witty and naughty.

KATE. Tick tick tick tick. How's your wife?

ANDY. We used to court here, by this river – the 'smelly'.

KATE. A clever girl that, her head screwed on.

ANDY. Our womenfolk aren't social plotters, you know – not calculating, like your lot.

KATE. Nonsense! A woman will calculate no matter which class she comes from – or would you like to sell me the myth of the working-class mother tending her brood of hard-working sons and plain-speaking daughters? Still, I suppose it's good for the biography. Andrew Cobham, a man of simple tastes – great though he was he constantly returned to the bosom of the common people and his simple wife.

ANDY. My house is in order, my food is cooked, and my children are loved and cared for.

KATE. Yes, well, it sounds as though you have a good house-keeper. Only she sent you out with a button missing from your shirt. Our housekeeper wouldn't put anything back in the drawer without looking for tears and lost buttons.

ANDY. I'm sure that when the costume you're wearing loses its buttons you'll just buy a new one.

KATE. I didn't buy this one, I made it.

ANDY. You have hobbies then – how clever.

KATE. Not clever at all – I hate making things. If I had my way I'd have everything made for me, I can't bear manual labour, but it relieves my boredom and softens my temper.

ANDY. Are you in love with me?

KATE. Yes.

ANDY. God knows why I asked. (*Pause.*) Now look at that city down there. What gangrenous vision excited the men who built that, I wonder?

KATE. There's a war coming soon.

ANDY. Soon?

KATE. Two or three years.

ANDY. That soon?

KATE. Unless I've drawn the wrong conclusions from what I saw.

ANDY. You went in cold blood, parading as a Nazi sympa-thizer, admiring the work of concentration camps?

KATE. What matter how cold my blood was? I needed to know. I told them I was a journalist and went to find out.

ANDY. You're a ruthless woman, Kate Ramsay.

KATE. Oh you're such a bore with your half-hearted humanity.

36

Ruthless! My so-called ruthlessness has now equipped me to save thousands. (*Pause.*) Besides, can I help it if I look like the master race?

ANDY. I don't know why we fought for sex equality, so help me I don't.

KATE. Rest on no laurels, my dear, it hasn't happened yet. Do you know I once asked Jake to take me to his union branch meeting and he spent all evening with his tail between his legs – I embarrassed him.

ANDY. Dressed with your sort of ostentatiously simple elegance, I don't wonder.

KATE. Simple elegance is not ostentatious – unless you're not used to it. Or would you have me go to his branch meeting dressed in tweeds or those nasty cotton frocks from the stores? I don't believe in wearing cloth caps to earn love from the masses. (*Pause.*) Andy – would you consider standing for councillor?

ANDY. If only you didn't make politics sound like a dirty job.

KATE. How touchy he is.

ANDY. What the hell do I know of local politics?

KATE. You could get in – you're trusted.

ANDY (*moving off*). God help me, Kate, I don't want to go into into local politics – I'm an architect; they should be screaming for me to build their houses, down on their bloody knees for me.

KATE (*following*). Singing hallelujahs for you.

ANDY. Aye, well, aye! Singing hallelujahs for me.

(*They've gone.*)

Scene 9

Andy's study. It is the year 1936.
Empty.

37

STONEY *staggers in pretending to be blind.* JESSIE *follows him with a tea tray.*

STONEY. Where is he, where's the man? Take me to him, let me feel him. (*Feels a chair.*) Andy? Ah master, safe and sound, still with us. God be praised.

JESSIE. The most irreverent priest I know. God'll have stern things to tell thee, lad.

STONEY. He's still got his wooden leg.

JESSIE. Get off your knees, fool – your childhood's passed.
    (PAUL *enters.*)

PAUL. Is the reverend bloody father still playing games?
    (PAUL *and* STONEY *help themselves to tea, they are 'at home'.*)

STONEY. Is Andy still with the council?

PAUL. How long does a council meeting go on for, for God's sake?

JESSIE. You should know, you've covered them often enough.

PAUL. Is he going to stand for council again?

JESSIE. No, he's not. He'll finish this term of office and then go into practice on his own. Two minor building projects is all he's pushed through and he says it's not worth it.

PAUL. I see they're writing about his schemes in the *Architects' Journal*.

JESSIE. That's what you're here to talk about.

STONEY. Aye, Andy and his cities; we've been summoned.

JESSIE. That's right, boys, you've been summoned. He has his answers.

STONEY (*quoting Andy*). 'What would you chuck out, have done with? What new things would you put there?'

PAUL. 'There it is, all virgin, a new piece of land, lovely, green, rich, what would us do with it?'

STONEY. 'Private industry? Have done with it. Let the unions and the co-ops take over – think what we could do with the profits.'

38

PAUL. 'Politicians are men we hire to mend roads and tend to
the sewers.'

STONEY. 'The Prime Minister is an accountant. Give the city
to its artists and teachers.'

JESSIE. He has his answers.

STONEY. Aye, we know them.

(*Sounds of* ANDY *approaching and arguing with someone
else. It is* SMITHY, *chairman of the local Labour Party.*)

SMITHY. And you must debate it, Andy, you, in public, and
you know it.

PAUL. What is it, Andy?

ANDY. Jake – the bloody fool.

PAUL. What is it?

SMITHY. I'm chairman of this city's Labour Party –

PAUL. Aye –

SMITHY. Thirty years in the movement –

PAUL. Aye, aye.

SMITHY. I've seen it before –

PAUL. Will you give over rambling and –

SMITHY. If I ramble, Paul, then that's my pace, let me make
my own pace. It may be slow and maybe I'm not as
brilliant as some of you, but my political experience tells
me no one'll follow a divided party.

PAUL. What's agitating him, Andy?

SMITHY. Local elections, that's what's agitating me. Next
week we've got local elections and in a year's time general
elections and Jake Latham's splitting the party.

PAUL. Smithy –

SMITHY. At my own pace, Paul, please, at my own pace.
Labour Party Conference last year voted to give more
power to the League of Nations so's the Nazis could be
prevented from growing – right? And now there's a split
in the party and Jake is among those who've turned against
the party's decision to support economic sanctions – even

39

though we all know it might lead to war.

PAUL. Against? On the eve of elections?

SMITHY. Who'll vote for us now? Thirty years in the movement – split after split – a party of individuals and eccen-
trics. Everyone shooting their mouths off in different
directions. Bloody intellectuals!

STONEY. Well, Andy?

SMITHY. No discipline, that's what I can't understand, no
discipline.

STONEY. Politics is your game now – here's your first big
dilemma: eve of poll and your closest friend has decided to
take a stand on his own.

SMITHY. He can take whatever stand he likes but not after he's
allowed policy to be made, not after he's continued to
stand as Area Chairman on that policy. (*Pause.*) Andy, you
– you must argue it out, at the next meeting, with Jake,
before the elections, I'll get every delegate to pack the hall.

PAUL. Don't be a fool, Smithy – you can't ask Andy to attack
Jake in public, not old friends you can't.

SMITHY. Old friends, old friends! We're all old friends, sloppy
bloody old friends. The movement can burn and you
wouldn't care so long as we was old friends together.

ANDY. I'll talk to him.

SMITHY. No Andy. I want it debated. I'm in the chair and I'll
see –

ANDY. I'll talk to him, I tell you.

STONEY. And your plans, Andy? For the new cities? Your
answers?

ANDY. Aye, the new cities, well they'll have to wait. There's
another bloody war coming up. They'll have to wait.

Scene 10

ANDY's *study some days later.*

JAKE *and* ANDY.

JAKE. Perhaps I should have told you. Of all people I should have told you.

ANDY. Fool.

JAKE. Old, Andy, I'm an old man. I don't always feel inclined to discuss every thought.

ANDY. Then stand down, old men should stand down.

JAKE. Old men should, should they?

ANDY. Don't play with me now, Jake. Stand down.

JAKE. Old men. So we fight, do we?

ANDY. I shall state what I feel to be right.

JAKE. Oh, Andy lad, how you do sound pompous at times. You don't have to be evasive with me. I ask you, we fight – do we?

ANDY. Hasn't Kate told you? Haven't you understood what Kate has told you? The Nazis have burnt the books of their poets – their poets, Jake.

JAKE. You know Kate is returning to Europe?

ANDY. I know it.

JAKE. 'I look like the master race,' she said, 'and I can speak fluent German. No better qualifications for a secret agent, you know.'

ANDY. It'll satisfy her need for drama, she'll love it.

JAKE. What'll you do when the war is over?

ANDY. Damn the war – damn you and the war.

(*Enter* JESSIE *with tea.*)

JAKE. Perhaps the war will clear a path for you – you and your cities.

ANDY. Jake, don't oppose me at the meeting.

JAKE. Don't?

ANDY. I don't want to fight my friends.

JAKE. You shouldn't saddle yourself with friends whose opinions you don't share.

ANDY. Don't oppose me, Jake, I'm weary of battling.

JAKE. Weary already?

ANDY. You don't think I enjoyed those council battles?

JAKE. It's you who should stand down perhaps.

(ANDY *is silent.*)

Aye, then we'll fight. It'll be a good lesson for thee. I'll not stay to tea, lass. Look after him.

(JAKE *leaves.*)

JESSIE. You can't, Andy – not Jake. That's a long friendship.

ANDY. Why do you always remind me of the things I know? Is my shirt ready?

JESSIE. It's pressed, there.

ANDY. Pressed? This collar? Pressed?

JESSIE. Collars are difficult, they never press straight.

ANDY. And there's a button missing. Time and again I've asked you – never put anything back without checking for tears and loose buttons. Now I shall be late.

JESSIE. There's others.

ANDY. No, I'll make do.

JESSIE. You're snapping, Andy.

ANDY. Snap? Do I? I didn't ever think I'd be a grumpy old man.

JESSIE. Thirty – old?

ANDY. It's a bad age, thirty. At twenty-nine you're still a young man; at thirty, well it's a halfway point between there and never.

JESSIE. I suppose everyone will be there.

ANDY. Yes.

JESSIE. Will you come back afterwards – the two of you?

ANDY. Probably.

JESSIE. Shall I make food?

42

ANDY. Food we'll have had. Just tea, your cake and some strong tea.

JESSIE. It won't be a vicious argument, will it, Andy?

ANDY. I shall state what I feel to be right.

JESSIE. Of course.

ANDY. You don't think that's pompous, do you; you never think anything I say is pompous – but it is. Jake's right. I never thought I'd be pompous.

JESSIE. Grumpy and pompous – all at thirty, my!

ANDY. Oh God, Jessie, shall us ever build cities? Shall us ever stop wasting energy and build those cities?

JESSIE. No time is waste, Andy.

ANDY. Yes, waste.

JESSIE. It's all a time of growing, lad.

ANDY. Waste.

JESSIE. Growing, growing, it's a time of growing, believe me.

ANDY. Waste! Waste! Waste!

Scene 11

It's a large meeting, some months later. The debate is in progress. Centre is chairman, SMITHY. Left is JAKE, right is ANDY. (Note: The platform should not face the audience.)

JAKE. ... God knows how it was done. I don't know how it was done. The degree to which we can be fooled sometimes leads me to despair and despise the class from which I come.

And now again, in 1936, the same humbugging machinery is in operation, the same appeal to our patriotism is being made. Do we sharpen our knives again? Is that our answer? Every time, is that going to be our answer? Don't you know what we've created in these last hundred years? An international movement capable of raising a finger and saying yes or no to every important issue confronting the world today.

Why did we create it? To raise our wages from one shilling to one and a penny an hour? Is that all?

I am aware that if we do not fight this war then our civilization will enter into terrible times. Terrible times. I know this – I've not loaded the argument on my side, if anything I've done the opposite. But what can an old man do except say the things he passionately believes? Old men have no need to lie, it's all over for them – the days of tactic, of political manoeuvre, of patchwork. What should an old man say but the thoughts which all his life he's felt were perhaps too irresponsible to utter? Irresponsible? It is said that people like me are irresponsible. I don't know, my friends, I do not know. I feel I will never know the answer – your vote for my resolution calling a halt to this useless rush to re-arm must be my answer; what you decide will decide me.

But,

I want to say this. Defeat doesn't matter. In the long run all defeat is temporary. It doesn't matter about present generations, but future ones always want to look back and know that someone was around acting on their beliefs. I can only tell you that I believe you were intended to live on this earth at peace with one another – if some people do not allow us to do this then I am ready to stand as the early Christians did and say – this is my faith, this is where I stand and if necessary, this is where I will die.

(*Tumultuous applause.*)

ANDY. Andrew Cobham, secretary Number 7 Branch. I want you to know that the man I shall be attacking is the one to whom I owe most of my intellectual development; in this way you will know how deeply I feel about the issue. This

44

meeting must not be influenced either by sentiment or personal attachment. Let me remind you that when Jake Latham says what he has said today it is rather late to say it and I hope you will carry no resolution of an emergency character simply to help a man with a conscience like Jake's decide what he ought to do. How he should act is a matter for his own conscience. For Jake Latham to hawk his conscience around for other people to absolve is not only confusing the issue but is basically dishonest. Because, if in the end Jake Latham is going to act on the basis of individual conscience, then he had no right at any time to assume a position of leadership.

JAKE. I've always declared my position.

ANDY. But you remained in office knowing you were leading hundreds of people who in the end you would have to abandon on grounds of private conscience.

VOICES. We asked him to stay!

Thank God he did! etc.

ANDY. You asked him to stay! You asked him to stay! For love? For affection? There was a time when you prevented this man from going to the top of his movement because of some private affair that offended your puritanical morals and now you declare love for him? Why? Because he's shaking with the pain of his own conscience? When your father has an accident do you sit and croon about your love for him or do you ignore your love and face the fact there are hospitals that can cure him? Love or facts? There is a time for love when facts are faced. This is no moment to be seated at the feet of self-styled saints.

VOICES. Shame!

Withdraw!

He's more of a saint than you'll ever be.

ANDY (raising his voice above the cries). I tell you, I tell you – if you want Jake Latham to become a saint then let me make

45

it easier for you by lighting the faggots for his martyrdom.
(*Stunned silence.*)
Facts. Facts. It's too late for sentiment and, just as you,
I'm sick at heart that this is so.
Now,
let us begin. The argument is that this will be another war
which in the end will serve the interests of those who rule.
Facts:
In every fascist state it is the Labour movement that has
been attacked; who fondly thinks that in defeat it will not
happen here?
The argument is for unity of Labour's International Move-
ment to prevent this war.
Facts:
Jake Latham is the man who calls for unity, but look – he
takes a stand that cracks the very solidarity he wants.
How dare he argue then for unity?
The argument is that in a war we should reply by paralys-
ing every nation with a strike.
Facts:
Who will strike? The unions are destroyed in most of
Europe. Who's left?
Confronted with these facts do we continue speaking glibly
about what could be achieved by strike in the event of war?
There only ever was one answer – the international control
of the seas and an economic pact throughout the world
which would control the source of our raw materials. That
was an answer, at the time, the right time. Now, it's too
late. I'm sorry, Jake Latham, saint, or no saint, it's too late.
Those who can't accept the movement's policy must take
a course that is their own – but not, I tell you, not inside
this movement.

(*Applause, starting slowly, mounting to crescendo.*

ANDY, JAKE *and* SMITHY *step down.* SMITHY *attempts to*

shake ANDY's *hand.* ANDY *turns his back.* SMITHY *leaves.*)

ANDY. Damn you, Jake Latham, you've made me do damage to myself again.

JAKE. Did you imagine it was facts that swayed that gathering to your side, Andy? When you stand up and say you're sick at heart, you win a sentimental point and all your pleas to them to take no heed of sentiment are waste. And when you say you owe a debt to someone you attack, then you have made another sentimental point which all your pleading to ignore will not cut out. And it was fair to say I 'hawked' my conscience all around? Was that the action of a friend?

ANDY. You're saying I betrayed a friend?

JAKE. Be careful of your cities, that's what I'm saying. One day you're old and you say right things – but it's all too late; that's what I'm saying.

ANDY. Will you come back with me now? Jessie has cake and tea ready.

JAKE. Cake and strong tea, is it? Aye, let's go. I'll go with you home.

(*The stage slowly comes to dark. The sound of an air-raid siren is heard; planes approach, bombs fall, flames crackle – the war has come and must be past in these few seconds until –*)

Scene 12

The Cathedral.

JESSIE *is standing on a tomb in a high state of excitement.*

The others are preparing to wander off to continue sketching.

JESSIE. What kind of cities shall we build, Andy? Paul, what kind of cities?

ANDY (*moving off, looking round*). Cities of light and shade,

Jessie, with secret corners. Cities of surprise and comfort, with wide streets and twisting lanes.

PAUL. Cities for lovers, Jessie, and old men and crawling children.

ANDY. Cities that frighten no one, with warm houses, low arches and long alleys.

PAUL. Cosy cities, Jessie, family cities.

STONEY. Cities for crowds and lone wolves.

PAUL. Cities full of sound for the blind and colour for the deaf.

STONEY. Cities that cradle the people who live there.

PAUL. That sing the praises of all men, Jessie.

JESSIE (*rising to the mood of prophecy and catechism*). Who will help you, my ragged-arsed brothers?

ANDY. The new Labour!

JESSIE. The same as asked you to build the new houses?

PAUL. Aye. After we've built the houses we'll go to the Council Chambers and we'll say, 'We've come again, we've built the houses and now your ragged-arsed sons have come to build you your cities.'

JESSIE. Shall us be proud?

ANDY. Aye, us'll be proud – they'll be proud. 'Build us cities,' they'll say, they'll command. 'Build us cities of light.'

ACT TWO

Scene 1

A Town Hall chamber.
It is the year 1947.
ANDY *and* CHAIRMAN *of local town planning.*

CHAIRMAN. We're not interested, we can't be interested. You must be mad to imagine my committee would ever have given it a thought. New cities? New ones? When we've made promises about post-war slum clearances?

ANDY. Slum clearances? Patchwork! All over the country bits and pieces of patchwork. I've done it.

CHAIRMAN. Rooms, give 'em that – to eat and sleep, give 'em that. Four walls, to keep out wind and rain – that's what we promised and that's what we'll give 'em.

ANDY. Patchwork, patchwork.

CHAIRMAN. People owning all their own houses? Workers owning their own factories? This Labour Council wouldn't last five minutes if we proposed a lunatic scheme like that.

ANDY. You sold us different dreams while we were at war, mister.

CHAIRMAN. Yes, yes, dreams – I know all about the spirit of 1945. Some intellectual loud-mouth does a bit of dreaming during wartime and we're left to give it shape and practice in peacetime.

ANDY. And what a botch you make of it.

CHAIRMAN. Don't be cheeky wi' me, Cobham. You're a respected man now, a famous architect, a war hero and all that, but don't battle me with your insults. I've been in the game too long –

ANDY. Aye, and don't you talk like it, too.

CHAIRMAN. I'm twice your age and I've been a bloody founder of this local Labour Party, a founder –

D   49

ANDY. – and you act like you're the only ones can inherit the good bloody earth! You think you've got the prerogative on suffering, don't you? I can see you all, spending your time boasting who was out of work longest in the good old days. Your lot wear your past so bloody smugly, my God –

CHAIRMAN. Right now, lad, be easy. You mustn't think because I'm firm that I don't see –

ANDY. I mean, what's the difference? What's the bloody difference? The opposition used to give the same sort of answer – only they offered round the drinks meanwhile.

CHAIRMAN. Oh, lad, I'm sorry, here, I'm sorry, of course, what'll you have?

ANDY. My! Look how you rush to copy them.

CHAIRMAN. Now listen to me, Mr Cobham –

ANDY. Why not offer me tea, a good cup of strong working-class tea.

CHAIRMAN. Well tea then, tea, lad – MAISY! Two teas, luv!

ANDY. Now why should you offer me tea? That's why you and your puritanical colleagues will never do this city proud, you're such cheapskates. Give me a whisky, Mr Comrade Chairman Jackson, I'm worth it. You get used to the idea that it's worth paying for what it's worth paying for! MAISY, we don't want any teas! A good whisky, a double one, 'cos you'll go a long way to find an architect like me in this city.

CHAIRMAN. Not in all my years have I been so –

ANDY. Socialist? Socialist Council, you call yourself?

CHAIRMAN. MR COBHAM –

ANDY. Don't stop me, I'm in full flight. Socialist! 'Four walls, Mr Cobham, to keep out wind and rain, just somewhere to eat and sleep, Mr Cobham.' Practical men? I spit 'em! Facts, Mr Jackson: when I told this council years ago that Floral Houses should come down or they'd fall down, the reply was 'Nonsense! We've got schools to build, can't afford it.' Well, they fell and the new school was missing ten children. Facts: the last Labour Housing Chairman approved designs for houses that now let in so much water half the inhabitants are in sanatoriums suffering from TB. And you, even you built a block of flats on top of an underground river. You practical boys are so mean-spirited that in half a century you'll turn us into one great sprawling slum. Even your whisky's cheap.

CHAIRMAN. You're asking us to change our whole society for God's sake.

ANDY. Hallelujah!

(*Pause.*)

CHAIRMAN. You're married, aren't you, Cobham?

ANDY. Aye.

CHAIRMAN. How many children?

ANDY. Three.

CHAIRMAN. Insured?

ANDY. Eh?

CHAIRMAN. Is everyone insured?

ANDY. Insured? What are you on about, insured? I'm talking about a new kind of city and all he can talk about is insurance.

CHAIRMAN. I'm not a fool, Cobham, and you listen, you listen, you listen to me. Patchwork? Slum clearance – patchwork? Right. I agree. And what's more I agree for your reasons: the intrusion of a little bit of order in the midst of chaos. Useless. I agree. Patchwork. I agree. Because one day the chaos will overwhelm the tiny bit of order, won't it? Very clever. You know it, you're not a fool. A bit romantic, maybe, but so what, a good quality, a fault on the right side as they say.

But think, think, Cobham, your cities, those beginnings of the good life. Think. You've not let us fool you, so you won't fool yourself, surely? *You* know why the cities won't work – them's also patchwork. Them's also a little bit of order in the midst of chaos. Bits of oasis in the desert that the sun dries up, that's all. Do you like my poetry? I can spin the right phrase out when I try, you know. I can toss a metaphor or two when I want. You lads don't have the prerogative on passion, Cobham, no more than we've the prerogative on suffering.

Now them's thoughts for you, them's real thoughts for you, you think on 'em.

　(Pause.)

ANDY. Whether you stonewall, whether you legislate, whether you lobby, argue, deceive or apply your lovely reasonable sanity, the end is the same. A cheapskate dreariness, a dull caution that kills the spirit of all movements and betrays us all – from plumber to poet. Not even the gods forgive that.

Scene 2

The riverside some days later.

ANDY *and* KATE.

KATE. And when you told him that not even the gods will forgive him what did he say?

ANDY. He'd take the risk.

KATE. And so?

ANDY. And so – nothing!

KATE. Nothing?

ANDY. Slum clearances, that's what I'll do. Patch it up. Crutches, give 'em crutches.

KATE. How easily you've inherited the language of your critics.

ANDY. Well what do you expect? '*They'll* command us,' we used to say. '*They'll* command *us*! Look at us, what betrayed ragged-arses we are; weaned on passion. Poor old passion! Poor, bloody, old passion! And for what?
(*Pause.*)

KATE. Andy, you want to do it alone don't you?

ANDY. Are you mad?

KATE. Andy, why don't you do it alone?

ANDY. The odds are too great.

KATE. That's no reason.

ANDY. I'm too old.

KATE. That's no reason.

ANDY. Too tired, too wise.

KATE. No reason, no reason at all. Now, let's begin again. Andy, why don't you do it alone?
(*He refuses to answer.*)
Yes, well perhaps you're right. The idea of a Golden City is dreary anyway.

ANDY. I must have been mad.

KATE. Who ever believes a call to arms?

ANDY. Don't tempt me. It's just too easy to tempt me.

KATE. Who ever heard of enthusiasm commanding attention?

ANDY. I tempt myself all the time.

KATE. There's something so much more significant about despair, isn't there?

ANDY. I'm just the sort of fool to be tempted.

KATE. You could always say you tried, very honourable; all the glory of good intentions without the actual struggle.

ANDY. You're becoming a nagger and that's what I'd become if I did it alone, a righteous old nagger.

KATE. All right, Andy, I'm going home.

ANDY. Going? Don't I amuse you?

KATE. Perhaps you'd like to stand on your head for me?

ANDY. Aye, that if you like.

KATE. Andy, I'm tired of timid lads who laugh at themselves. I'm tired of little men and vain gestures. I have a need, O God how I have a need to see someone who's not intimidated. Who's not afraid to be heroic again.

ANDY. Kate, the hero is a bore.

KATE. As you wish. (*Makes to leave.*)

ANDY. The hero is a sign, you old nag you – a sign of failure.

KATE. Ah! Failure, that's what you're afraid of?

ANDY. Yes, of course I'm afraid of failure – petrified. A golden city is doomed to failure, don't you understand? One city, six cities, a dozen – what difference? It's all patchwork – like the chairman said. There'd be plenty wanting to help me patch up – oh, yes – and then when it was done they'd heave a sigh of relief that they'd managed to stave off the real revolution for yet another century. Why shouldn't I be afraid?

KATE. Then I ask you, since the bloody revolution you would like cannot be achieved – what is there left worth doing? (*Pause.*)

ANDY. Who would build the city with me?

KATE. Your friends – where are they?

ANDY. Stoney, Paul? The war lost us. It would be like digging up the dead.

KATE. Then do that, wake the dead.

ANDY. I haven't the language of heroism, Kate.

KATE. Then forge it.

ANDY. From what? The words of politicians?

KATE. Forge it.

ANDY. From the old poets?

KATE. Forge it.

ANDY. From the pages of dead pamphlets?

KATE. Forge it, forge it.

ANDY. The language of heroism is a dead language, Kate. You need to be desperate to forge it.

KATE. A desperate language? Forge it.

ANDY. A desperate language breeds desperate deeds for God's sake.

KATE. Then I ask you again – what else is there left worth doing?

(*Long pause.*)

ANDY. You know, recently I attended a May Day demonstration – a dreary march, from one street corner to another. *There* were the usual half-hearted banners and *there* were the isolated hand-claps from the handful of people on the pavements; and in front of the march, sure enough, there was our foremost political leader of the left, giving his uncertain smiles and nods to empty streets and embarrassed children. And when the marchers arrived at their destination this foremost political leader of the left stood up and made a speech about pensions and housing and the balance of trade. And suddenly, out of the crowd, a young lad shouted, 'Inspire us!' Now, think of him, Kate. My God, inspire us.

Scene 3

ANDY's *study, some weeks later.*

PAUL, STONEY *sit in uneasy silence.* KATE *stands by.*

PAUL. Well, inspire us then.

ANDY. I see, you're going to make it difficult, are you?

PAUL. Why not? You've dragged us from the peace of our homes, now pay for it.

STONEY. You've become aggressive, Paul. It doesn't suit you.

PAUL. And you've become senile. I've no patience with people who still think they can advance human progress.

KATE. That's a dreary piece of cynicism. Is that the level of your disillusionment?

STONEY. I don't suppose Andy expected the joy of an old comrades' reunion – did you, Andy?

ANDY. Now that you're here I'm not sure what I expected.

PAUL. Well, you'd better hurry up and find out, hadn't you?

STONEY. We're not being gracious, I'm feeling.

(*Awkward silence.*)

ANDY. Look at you both! You'd love to help me build these cities but you're too mean to show it. Look at you! Shrinking your poor little souls behind those comfortable disenchantments. How you wail and you whimper and you whine. (*Mocking.*) 'I've no patience with people who still think they can advance human progress.'

(*Pause.*)

PAUL (*reluctantly*). How much will it cost?

ANDY (*jumping to it*). A city for a hundred thousand inhabitants would take fifteen years to complete and cost £156,000,000.

STONEY. £156,000,000?

ANDY. That means every man must find £1,560 for everyone in his family – to pay not merely for their houses but for all the public buildings as well.

STONEY. You've been working hard.

ANDY. I've got a questionnaire here, I've worked one out, we'll ask each person what kind of a city he wants. Participation! We'll involve them, a real community project, a real one!

STONEY. And our roles? Each of us here? The part we play, tell us those. We're a bit of a battered lot, us. Look at us.

PAUL. What must we do now? Search our souls for some sort of credentials?

STONEY. Aye, in a way, credentials – a sort of worthiness.

KATE. The reverend Dean wants to know if we're good people, don't you, dear?

STONEY. Yes, I do – is that wrong?

KATE. So look at us, Andy. What do you see? A good journalist who might have made a good poet but didn't. Partner
number one – frustrated! Terrible credentials. Go home,
Paul Dobson. A minister, a religious administrator, a
lover of love who can't bring himself to admit how dulled
he is by his experience of it – partner number two.
Terrible, terrible credentials – back to your desk, Reverend
Jackson. Me? A daughter of impoverished aristocracy, a
woman with a constant sneer in her voice, unloved and
with no respect for the will of the people. Why don't we
all go home, Reverend Jackson?
  (*Silence.*)

STONEY. Where is Jessie, Andy? Why isn't she with us? She
was part of us, once. Why does she stay in the kitchen?

KATE (*impatiently*). Yes, where is your housekeeper? Why isn't
your housekeeper asked to contribute to the discussions?

STONEY. See what I mean, Andy? She could never build such
a city as you want, never! If I were Andy I'd have slapped
the arse off you for that, but good and hard.

ANDY. Ignore it, Stoney. We don't have to be saints to have
dreams.

STONEY. I cannot build your city with the sneers of a dying
aristocracy ringing in my ears.

KATE. I'm not a dying aristocracy – I'm classless.

STONEY. Classless? The common man would smell you decay-
ing a mile off.

KATE. The common man! What a fraudulent myth – the
glorious age of the common man! My God, this is an age
of flabbiness, isn't it? You know, Stoney, it's not really the
age of the common man, it's the age of the man who is
common, and if it's unforgivable that my class has pro-
duced the myth, then you should weep, yes weep, that
your class has accepted it.

Haven't you noticed how we pat you on the head at the

57

mere sign of intelligence? 'He reads,' we say; 'how quaint, give him newspapers with large print', but we keep the leather-bound volumes of poets on our shelves. Haven't you noticed the patronizing way we say, 'He's artistic, how touching – give him pottery classes and amateur theatricals' – but the masters continue to hang on our walls and the big theatres are our habitat, not yours.

ANDY. Our homes are made of brick with crisp square lines and fully equipped kitchens.

KATE. – but ours are the Georgian mansions out in the fields and we have rooms for our guests while you, you have just enough for your family.

PAUL. We're well fed and there's ample roast beef at home.

KATE. – yes, Paul. But we know the taste of caviare, don't we? And there are vintage wines on our tables.

STONEY (*catching on*). And in this day of the man who is common and drives his Austin and Ford we think we're equal to any man.

KATE. – but we have the Bentley and the Rolls and keep quiet.

STONEY. So?

KATE. So, because we need to perpetuate the myth that class differences are past, we pat his head and consult the man who is common in the name of the common man. Questionnaires, Andy? (*Holding one up.*) Is this what *you* imagine makes it the age of the common man? This? (*Reading.*) 'For the people who plan to inhabit the new cities so that we may know better how to build them.' Fancy! Architects asking laymen how to build a city. Why should the man who buys his city know how to build it? Why shouldn't we turn to you for our homes, to the poet for his words, to the Church for its guidance? Participation? It's a sop, dear, to ease your conscience. Tear them up – be brave, you know well enough how you want those cities built – shall we tear them up?

(ANDY *pauses – then smiles and nods at* KATE. KATE *tears up the questionnaire.*)

PAUL. But Andy's not even convinced himself. It's all patch-work, he says. How can he persuade others of a glory he doesn't believe in himself?

ANDY. If I decide to build those cities, then I'll forget they could ever have been regarded as patchwork, I'll ignore history.

PAUL. And what makes you think we'd ever agree to this massive piece of self-deception.

ANDY. Paul, if I'd come to you with brave declarations and the cry of an easy Utopia would you have believed that? (*Pause.*)

PAUL. No, I'd not have believed that.

ANDY. Then what else is there left worth doing? The alterna-tive was that complete revolution we all used to talk about, but – there's no situation that's revolutionary, is there? Face it, all of you. There – is – no – revolutionary – situation.

(ANDY *challenges them all but there is only silence.*)

Then let's begin.

In the way you build a city you build the habits of a way of life in that city – that's a fact. Six Golden Cities could lay the foundations of a new way of life for all society – that's a lie, but that's the lie we're going to perpetuate, with our fingers crossed.

STONEY. And the method?

ANDY. Simple. There are architects and town planners through-out the country who I know would form six working committees to find sites and draw up plans.

PAUL. And the initial cost?

ANDY. Each committee would need £5,000 to open up offices for the first year. A year of planning, building models, battling authorities and finding the first 16,000 inhabitants.

I've already set aside £5,000 for our first offices.

STONEY. And the inhabitants? How do you begin to look for them?

ANDY. When the whole scheme is announced in the press there'll be thousands of applications – I know it. We'll invite the applicants to attend a Monday Meeting which we'll conduct weekly for perhaps the first five years – maybe more. And at these meetings the plans will be explained in detail and we can select the right age groups and create the correct balance of professions.

PAUL. And the money? How will the first money come in?

ANDY. Instalments. Before the work can begin, each family will have to start paying instalments on their house – no, their city! It'll take three years to accumulate sufficient capital to start building.

STONEY. And how long will it take before they can move in?

ANDY. Five years, five years for the first phase of building.

STONEY. Five years? Three years to start and five years of building? Eight years, Andy. You're asking people to wait eight years to move into a house.

PAUL. Don't be so dull-witted, Stoney. They'll be waiting eight years for their own city, more than their own house.

STONEY. It's paralysing.

PAUL. One last question – industry. The money for industry – who'll provide that?

ANDY. Industry. Aye, well, there lies the major battle.

Scene 4

The Cathedral.
PAUL *and* STONEY *are lying around in resting positions, listening to the story* ANDY *is telling* JESSIE.

ANDY. There was a man called Joseph Arch once, a farm
labourer from Warwickshire, born about 1850. And one
day three men called on him, in his house, and asked him
to be their leader. They wanted him to come that night
into a town called Wellingbourne; there was to be a meeting. They wanted, they told him, to get the local farm
labourers together and start a union directly. 'Oh,' he said,
'a union, is it? You'll have to fight hard for it and suffer
for it,' he said, 'you and your families,' he said. They told
him they knew that and they and their families were ready.
JESSIE. Did it succeed?
ANDY. No, it was smashed – but they'd begun, and once the
Combination Laws were repealed they stopped going
underground and started in earnest.
Now,
consider, it's only about sixty years later, just that, a lifetime only, and look – there's all those people, all that
organization, all those improvements. Now that strikes me
as an exciting story but no one seems to have seen what
happened. They know wages have gone up, they can see
improved housing and better working conditions, but no
one seems to have seen much else. It's like, it's like – how
should I tell you? – it's like some people who are stranded
on an island and a hundred miles away is the mainland, so
they must build a boat. Now they only want the boat too
carry them for a little way, for a short time; but as they
build it they sink holds and erect decks, they build cabins
and kitchens, they give it a polish and lots of sails and all
they do is travel a hundred miles from one piece of land to
another. But that's daft, isn't it? I mean, why don't they
seem to realize they could live on it, trade in it, travel right
across the world in it? 'No,' they say, 'we only wanted it
to go from the island to the mainland – that was its only
job.' So there is it, in the harbour, and they keep it polished,

waiting for another emergency – but that's all.

And I don't know –

but it seems to me that someone has to tell them – that that
ship can span every ocean there is, every ocean, look, and
reach all corners of the world. It seems to me – someone
has to tell them that.

Scene 5

The Trades Union Congress. It is the year 1948.

A back projection of the General Council who are listening to ANDY
addressing Congress.

ANDY *is alone on a rostrum.*

*A long cloth banner stretches behind him with the words ANNUAL
TRADES UNION CONGRESS.*

*At the base of the platform of the General Council is a decoration of
flowers.*

ANDY'*s recorded voice is heard immediately young Andy has
finished.*

Note: He must *not* address the next speech to the audience.

ANDY (*recorded*). ... and there it stays, in the harbour, and we
keep it polished, waiting for another emergency, and that's
all. But someone has to say it, sooner or later. Someone
has to say, 'Look, look at that ship, it's more than a raft,
it has sails. The wind can catch those sails and the ship can
span every ocean there is. It can span every ocean and reach
all corners of the earth.'

(*live*). Why did we build such a ship, with eight million
people aboard? To raise our wages every year by pennies?
To ensure that our offices are guarded by first-aid kits and
our factories have posh flush lavatories? Is that all? When,
with the lovely voice of all our energies we could command

the building of the most beautiful cities in the world. More
– the most beautiful world itself, I tell you.

Years ago, many years ago, when I first came into the
movement, at a time of scant employment, falling membership and apathy – a man asked a question. Some of you
will remember that man – Jake Latham, chairman then,
dead now. The movement had been alive for half a
century, half a hundred years of argument, and achievement, look; yet – the 1933 crisis came and apathy confronted him. 'What,' he asked, he was an old bewildered
man, 'what, since we have failed, is there that holds men
in a movement through all time? Any movement, not
even a movement – groups, a family, a community, a
civilization?' He had no answer. Tired – he was a tired, old
man.

But is this us? Old men? Tired old men? The most terrible
war in history is won – by us – we should be jubilant, we
should be singing. We should have answers and not be
doubled up by despair. Old men have no answers and when
old age is ours, then, then we can cry in bewilderment.
But now, our blood is young, we should cry – we know!
Old age laments, leave lamentations till the grave – *we*
know? *We* know what holds men in a movement through
all time – their visions. Visions, visions, visions! What
else? To fight for a penny more an hour for standing at the
lathe, our energies for only this? A movement built for
only this? The battle for our daily needs?

But men have minds which some good God has given so
we can tackle problems bigger than our daily needs, so we
can dream. Who dares to tell us we've no right to dream?
The dull and dreary men? Then tell the dull and dreary
men to crawl away.

I tell you,

this resolution now before you builds a dream. In the way

you shape a city you shape the habit of a way of life.
I tell you,
we have a city we can build, we *have* a city. We have a
city we can build out of whose contours comes the breath
of such a brave new world.
I tell you,
the dull and dreary men preach caution, caution is a kind
of fear.
The dull and dreary men breed apathy, apathy is a kind of
cancer.
But look, *we* have a city. The dull and dreary men, beware
– beware the dull and dreary men.
I tell you, look –
we have a city, we can have a city!

(*Fade in sounds and murmurs of a meeting. These sounds
carry through to the next scene to become the murmurs of the
first Monday Meeting.*)

Special Note

From here on begins the 'continuous' scene –
Scene 6 – that is to say, a scene taking us right to
the end of the play as one set dissolves rapidly into
another. It will cover many years and many situa-
tions and the purpose of proposing this method of
staging is to create a sense of purpose, bustle,
activity and – most important – growth and decay.
The long battle to build the city will begin and end
in this 'continuous' scene. Towards the end of each
situation (set), preparation will be going on for the
next situation (set), so that characters will turn
immediately from one phase of the development
to another. It must appear as one continuous move-

ment, slowly and inexorably unfolding – rather
like watching the painting of Dorian Gray slowly
change from a young man into an old and evil man
– as in the film.

Scene 6

Covering the years 1948–90 or thereabouts.
The Golden City offices.
This is the first of the 'Monday Meetings'.
'Monday Meetings' will continue as the years go by, and through
them we will build up a verbal image of the cities.
A board hangs in the background:
'MONDAY MEETING – FIRST WEEK'
PAUL *and* STONEY *have just addressed an audience.* KATE *is in*
attendance. The murmuring of the audience dies down.
QUESTIONER. Right! You've shaped the city. There are the
    plans, we've seen them, good! But now, a question. What
    about its spirit? The city's spirit – how will you shape
    that?
PAUL. Good question. A city's spirit, what will be the city's
    spirit? Look, look more closely at these plans. What do
    you see?
STONEY. Variety – that's what you see. Roads that are wide
    and alleys that ramble.
PAUL. Bold squares and intimate corners.
STONEY. There's colour in that city, and sound.
PAUL. And movement of line and patterns of mass.
STONEY. Not a frightening city, not intimidating.
PAUL. And its heart? What do you see as its heart? Industry
    may be a city's backbone but what should be a city's heart?
VOICE. A Town Hall?

STONEY. Look again – look more closely at these plans again. You can't seriously place a Town Hall at the city's heart – not a place where functionaries meet to organize our tax affairs and drainage problems.

PAUL. No. Our city's heart is its gardens, concert halls, theatres, swimming pools.

STONEY. Dance halls, galleries and meeting rooms.

PAUL. Restaurants and libraries, look – a rearrangement of priorities.

STONEY. And you can build it, over many years it's true, but you can build it. It's not been done before. No one's ever challenged men to pool their money and build their own city –

PAUL. – but it can be done.

(*At this point* ANDY *enters.* STONEY *and* KATE *turn to him.* PAUL *still addresses the audience.*) Or are we still afraid to re-arrange priorities?

KATE (*to* ANDY). You didn't turn up.

ANDY. How many came?

KATE. You didn't turn up.

ANDY. How many came I asked.

PAUL. Twenty.

KATE. The first of the Monday Meetings and you didn't turn up.

ANDY. You couldn't have understood, Kate, Jessie was ill.

KATE. Are you going to neglect this project every time there's an upset in the family?

ANDY. You forget yourself, Kate.

KATE. Answer me. Is this project to grow depending on the ups and downs of the Cobham household? Is it?

ANDY. The woman had a miscarriage for God's sake.

KATE. So? There are doctors to guard the sick, you have other things to guard.

ANDY. Thank you but I'll make my own decisions of priority.

KATE. Your decisions, any decisions you make, affect this project. I charge you again – your family is your family and your work is your work, and you have not the right, no right at all, to neglect a project involving so many for the sake of your own good life.

STONEY. And we were the ones just talking about the good life?

KATE. Don't! Don't confuse what we preach with what we must do.

ANDY. Kate!

KATE. Yes, cry 'Kate', but I warn you – those of us who build the Golden City can never live in it, never.

(*Silence.*

In this silence JESSIE *appears. She has brought* ANDY *a meal.*)

ANDY. We need more funds, the kitty is low.

KATE. Nurse that then. There's the illness, find funds.

(STONEY, KATE *and* PAUL *leave.*

It is ANDY'*s study.*

ANDY *opens a drawer, pulls out some drawings and tears them up.*)

JESSIE. What are you tearing? (*No answer.*) Don't be a fool, Andrew Cobham, what are you tearing? (*But she knows.*) Have you taken to tearing every design that your customer turns down? I thought it was the habit of architects to hold on to every last sketch.

ANDY. I can remember, when I first started on my own, I swore I would never erect a building I didn't approve of – I swore that.

JESSIE. Nor you haven't, have you?

ANDY. No, I haven't.

JESSIE. Well?

ANDY. Well, woman, you know what the cynics say – every man has his price; they must be right.

67

JESSIE. I always thought that cynicism didn't impress you.

ANDY. And it doesn't, but facts do and the fact is we've hardly any money left and my designs for the technical college have been turned down – too expensive.

JESSIE. Can't the project start paying you a salary now? You've been going a year –

ANDY. Now stop that. I've told you. The funds are low. The project and this household must live off the practice; that's why I built it.

JESSIE. Andrew Cobham, as the years go on it gets harder and harder to live with you. I'll not have you grunting and storming through this house because you're building a building you don't want to build. You, with a screaming and snapping head above what you are, is more than I can bear. We'll –

ANDY. A screaming and snapping head above what I am, eh?

JESSIE. It's not been a happy year that's gone, not a calm one. (*Pause.*)

ANDY. I'll build them anything they want, Jessie. And my City is my price.

(JESSIE *leaves. We hear the sound of applause.* ANDY *has just addressed a Monday Meeting. A number of people come to greet him. He chats with them as he prepares to go to the Ministry of Town and Country Planning.*)

ANDY. Right! We have a site. At last, after a year of searching, the first site for the first city has been found. And why? Because the number of people who've started to buy their own city has grown and everyone's started to take us seriously. They've had to: the money's coming in and that's a fact, that money is, a fact! Now – permission. One small council has offered us a site and the Ministry of Town and Country Planning must give permission to build. They must! They can't refuse! There's too much enthusiasm! Look at us – our hundredth Monday Meeting and our audiences have risen from twenty to six hundred and that's not the largest audience of applicants we've had, no! Not by a long road! Do you know this scheme has captured the imagination not only of this country but of countries throughout the world. Aye! Throughout the world! The Ministry will have to give its blessing, Tory though it is. And you know what we'll say to them? 'You'll have the finest planners in the land at work,' we'll say. 'We'll make such innovations that you'll find a dozen problems solved in one go.' They can't refuse. Look at the size of this meeting, consider the response, they can't refuse. Goodbye. Thank you.

(*They applaud him as he moves off. We are now in a corridor in the Ministry of Town and Country Planning. An* OFFICIAL *talks to* ANDY.)

OFFICIAL. Mr Cobham, it really was kind of you to come but believe me, there arrive at these offices, every day, half a dozen plans and schemes by lunatics who think they can solve our housing problems in an hour. Not that I dare imply you are a lunatic; we are all aware, even the Minister I'm sure, of your fine achievements as an architect – but Mr Cobham, I couldn't even begin to interest the Minister in such a scheme.

ANDY. But the land's no good to agriculture, it's not a beauty spot, we're not even asking you for the money. Permission – that's all, authority and a signature, at no price. We'll raise the costs, we're raising the costs –

OFFICIAL. And I don't want you to think it's because of the political implication – I know that's what you're thinking – it's not. A Ministry like this, unlike other ministries, has very little need to make political decisions, you know.

ANDY. Ah, I see, you're a classless ministry.

OFFICIAL. Yes, very aptly put, Mr Cobham, a classless ministry, yes, I like that. Good day.

ANDY. 'Yes, Mr Cobham, very aptly put, a classless ministry,
I like that.'

(KATE *appears*.)

KATE. That will teach you to work through office boys. Now
will you listen to me? With your reputation you're going
to meet the Minister.

(*A cocktail party is being prepared.*

Couples are wandering in.

ALFRED HARRINGTON, *an industrialist, whose party this is,*
steps up to ANDY *and* KATE, *offering them drinks*.)

HARRINGTON. I can't understand why you bother with small
officials. A man with your reputation should have demanded an interview with the Minister at once. Kate, why
did you let this man humiliate himself, you of all people?

KATE. Give him time, Alfred – we inherited our arrogance,
manipulating people comes easy to us.

HARRINGTON. She's tough is our Kate. You have a good ally,
Mr Cobham. We train them well but they stray. Look at
him, you think we're cynical, don't you? Not really. We
recognize ability. I'd be ashamed of myself if I allowed my
politics to blind me to ability. Ability coupled with guts is
irresistible. I don't like all the aspects of your Golden City,
but it's alive, dear boy, it's on fire. That's how I made my
fortune. I was on fire. To build dams across the rivers and
create the power for light seemed the most marvellous
thing in the world. I built forty of them, forty of them. My
own thin line of longitude, right around the globe. I was
on fire, like you. You're on fire, I can see your eyes flash!
And I can't resist. You'll see the Minister, I'll take you
there myself. My own thin line of longitude, right round
the globe.

(*As* HARRINGTON *moves off, 'fly in' additions to make it a*
more luxurious set for the Minister's cocktail party.

The Minister of Town and Country Planning – REGINALD

70

MAITLAND – *approaches* ANDY *and* KATE.)

MAITLAND. My dear Mr Cobham, it's an honour to meet you. Alfie Harrington has been speaking about your plans for ages – it's taken so long for us to meet, forgive me. Delighted, Miss Ramsay.

ANDY. It's very kind of you, Minister. I'm happy our project has gone so high as your good self.

MAITLAND. I know you imagine the Conservative ministries to be filled with hostile and reactionary diehards. It's a convenient image for you people on the left to hold, but the fact is we're all hard-working men, like yourself, and in order to stay in power we just have to have the country's interests at heart.

KATE. You'll see us then?

MAITLAND. But of course I shall see you; I'd be foolish, not to say rude, if I didn't make it my business to meet and listen to the nation's most able minds.

(HARRINGTON *reappears with a new drink.*)

ANDY. I'm concerned to see this city built, Minister, and since your permission is needed then I'll seek it and be grateful to receive it.

HARRINGTON. I bet your colleagues on the left won't be so grateful.

MAITLAND. The truth about the left, dear Cobham, is that it's dreary – face it – it's dull, self-righteous, puritanical, dreary. Always known what's wrong, of course; poverty, bad housing, long working hours – basic, simple criticisms. But it's taken us on the right to rectify those wrongs and a little more besides.

ANDY. Aye, under pressure, though.

MAITLAND. 'Aye,' he said. He still retains his dialect, charming, Cobham, charming. I'm delighted to have met you. Harrington?

(MAITLAND *moves off calling* HARRINGTON *to follow him.*)

KATE. He's patronizing you. Feel it? Well learn to feel it. Look at you, you want so much so badly that you leap at small favours. Raise your head and stop smiling or you'll begin to feel you've won the moment they start confiding those funny intimate stories about famous men of power.

(HARRINGTON *returns.*)

HARRINGTON. A shrewd man, that. Talks like a fool but acts with unparalleled toughness.

KATE. Of course he's shrewd, he knows we've found our first 25,000 inhabitants –

ANDY. – and deposited our first two million pounds.

KATE. There's a great deal of political gain in being benevolent to the left.

(*The party breaks up. Only* ANDY *is left. The thuds and scrapings heard from a building site now echo.*

STONEY *and* PAUL *join* ANDY *to address the 300th Monday Meeting.*)

ANDY. The building has begun. Enough money has been deposited and, ladies and gentlemen, the - building - has - begun. The land's drained. The huts are up. Water supplies within easy reach, road and rail communications –

PAUL. – and a countryside that's lovely, aye, lovely, lovely. Have you ever watched a city growing, ladies and gentlemen? Have you ever heard the hum of men building their own city? The walls rise and the flowers blossom.

ANDY. No endless rows of dreary houses but a grand design, of steeples and spires and levels of buildings that rise and fall.

STONEY. The walls rise and the flowers blossom; the rubble turns to roads.

ANDY. Sixteen hundred homes a year, ladies and gentlemen, that's our target.

PAUL. The rubble turns to roads and the dust from machinery settles –

ANDY. Sixteen hundred homes a year.

STONEY. – and the dust from machinery settles to reveal the slate and granite, the glass and cement and all the patterns men make for the pleasure of their living.

(*During these last seconds, three men take their places behind or near the desk. They are trade union leaders, members of the General Purposes Committee of the T.U.C.,* TED WORTHINGTON, BILL MATHESON, BRIAN CAMBRIDGE. PAUL *and* STONEY *leave.* ANDY *remains.*)

MATHESON (*reading from a small notebook*). ' … and the dust from the machinery settles to reveal the … ' – what's this? – slate? – 'the slate and granite', is it? 'The glass and cement and – and – all the patterns men make for the pleasure of their living.' Yes, that's it, 'all the patterns men make for the pleasure of their living.'

Yes. Pretty words. That's what I heard. I made notes, pretty words. The 300th Meeting it was, I went to listen. Pretty words you and your artist friends make.

CAMBRIDGE. All right, Bill, don't let's start off with sarcasm, we've got business to attend to.

MATHESON. Oh, I'm not being sarcastic. Andy knows me, don't you, Andy? Our unions have worked together many a time, haven't they? He knows me.

ANDY. Aye, I know you, Bill Matheson, and I know you resent me.

MATHESON. Resent you? Resent you? You're sensitive lad – too sensitive. Why should I resent you?

CAMBRIDGE. We've got business, I said; now settle.

MATHESON. Resent you? Yes, I do bloody resent you. The old chimera, the good ole Utopian Chimera rearing its irritating little head again.

ANDY. Do I have to listen to him, Brian?

CAMBRIDGE. Settle, I said.

MATHESON. There's one turns up every five years, the good old Utopian.

CAMBRIDGE. So help me, Bill, I'll turn you right out of the bloody door if you don't come to heel.

WORTHINGTON. He's a bit sloshed, is our Bill Matheson tonight, a bit over the eight.

CAMBRIDGE. Andy, I don't suppose I have to tell you why we've called you, do I, lad? The General Purposes Committee have to try and make order of these thousand and one resolutions before they're placed in front of Congress and we want to discuss the resolution your Union's putting up this year.

MATHESON. For the fourth year, mark you – that's persistence, that is, you and your draughtsmen's union. You must have a good membership behind you – wish I would get my buggers to support everything I propose.

ANDY. Start proposing the right things.

CAMBRIDGE. Now cut it out, lads, for Christ's sake. You're like a couple of bitchy females. (*To* ANDY.) I don't suppose we could persuade you to drop the resolution for this year, could we?

ANDY. No, you couldn't.

CAMBRIDGE. I mean, the more times it gets voted down the more bored the delegates get. You know how the lads are at Congress time – all sorts of bloody moods.

WORTHINGTON. It's staggering what you've done, Andy, staggering; but what about the other five cities? How's them? How's their committees going?

ANDY. Not as advanced as us, they're held back, waiting to see what happens to us. But –

MATHESON. Six cities? We must be mad to even discuss it with him. Six cities and he's asking the trade unions to finance the industry in all of them. You'd bankrupt us in six months.

ANDY. Not true – and you know it. At the rate at which they'd grow, the profits of our city could finance the industry of another. We've worked that out to the last detail – you've had the facts and figures for the last two years.

WORTHINGTON. Then why don't you build one city first and let the others follow?

MATHESON. Because one isn't enough. Because he wants the bloody glory of being a great revolutionary figure, don't you know? Haven't you heard the name he's got? The silent revolutionary – that's what the papers call him, the silent revolutionary.

WORTHINGTON. Ignore it, Andy, pass it by, answer my question – why not one city first?

ANDY. Because the prospect of six cities is the prospect of a real change. One becomes an experiment and experiments are patchwork. Remember Owen?

MATHESON. Yes, we do. Owen, Robert bloody Owen. Responsible for shattering what little trade unionism existed in those days – half a century wasted. We remember Owen all right.

WORTHINGTON. You're a fool, Bill Matheson, no education. You know your trouble, don't you? You really believe in profits.

MATHESON. Right! You're dead right. I've said it in public and I'll say it here. It's human, it's basic to the human mentality and the sooner we acknowledge it the sooner we'll get industrial peace. Owenites, that's what this lot is, Owenites, and they're going to shatter us again, I'm warning you, with their six Golden bloody Cities.

CAMBRIDGE. Don't be daft, Bill, he didn't ever seriously think he'd see six cities in his lifetime – did you, Andy? Not seriously. I mean that's a bit of bargaining power you've set up, isn't it? Give way on the other five and get your way on one? A bit of market bargaining, eh?

ANDY. Now watch it, Brian, you're patronizing me. I've had enough of being patronized. Just state your position and

75

ACT TWO

don't play politics. I'm a tough hand and I don't need softening up, just state your case.

CAMBRIDGE. You're right, Andy, you're right. You have to face so many nitwits on this committee that I use diplomacy when it's not needed. I should have known better, I'm sorry. I'll put it fair and square. For the last three years the General Council have advised Congress not to vote in favour of financing industry in the six cities. Now I'm not saying the General Council would ever recommend Congress to finance even one city, but it's bloody certain they can't consider six. If you want the scheme to make sense at all, then drop the other five.

ANDY. Drop them?

WORTHINGTON. Drop them, Andy, drop them. Build one of your cities and change the resolution accordingly. You don't stand a snowball's chance in hell of getting Congress to vote money for six.

ANDY. But for one?

CAMBRIDGE. But for one – I'll tell you frankly. Your project has focused attention on the constitutions of nearly every trade union in the country –

WORTHINGTON. – and nearly every constitution declares its fervent aim as being the final take-over of the means of production –

MATHESON. – which everyone has forgotten – thank God –

CAMBRIDGE. – until now.

ANDY. And now the General Council are embarrassed?

CAMBRIDGE. And now the General Council are embarrassed. The success you've been having has embarrassed them. They'll have to decide something.

ANDY. Can you guarantee they'll decide to recommend the financing of industry in one city?

CAMBRIDGE. Andy lad, for Christ's sake. You know I can't guarantee a thing like that.

76

ANDY. I'm really being pushed to the wall, aren't I?

CAMBRIDGE. I'd say you were being given a way out. You've now got the possibility of making one city work; before, there was the possibility of nowt. Think on it.

ANDY. I'll think on it.

WORTHINGTON. Andy, a resolution last year called for us to make an investigation into the type of housing estates that the Government and local councils are building. You're a personal friend of the Minister now, you'd be a great asset, would you sit on the committee?

MATHESON. That's it, give him another job, he's got broad shoulders, he's a bloody hero, a silent revolutionary – don't you know.

CAMBRIDGE. Come on, Bill, you're like an old grandmother these days, have another drink, put you out of everybody's way.

(MATHESON *and* CAMBRIDGE *leave.* WORTHINGTON *is halfway out as* PAUL, KATE, STONEY *take over the desk. It is the Golden City office.*)

WORTHINGTON. By the way, lad, have you ever stopped to consider what'll happen if industry couldn't be set up in the way you want it? You'd have six cities built and an army of unemployed smouldering in them. Think on it! (*Exits.*)

(ANDY *has his back to his three comrades.*)

KATE. So, they offered you the glory of another fact-finding committee, did they? Asked you to compromise with one voice and told you they loved and needed you with another. Clever. Clever boys. What was your answer? (*No reply.*) Andy, what was your answer? (*No reply.*)

PAUL. What did you tell them, Andy?

STONEY. You didn't agree?

KATE. Leave him answer.

PAUL. Andy, you didn't agree, did you?

77

KATE. Leave him answer, I say.

STONEY. But he couldn't agree. There's five other committees, they've got sites, all that work, those architects, all that money invested –

PAUL. They didn't promise to finance even one city.

STONEY. Haven't we compromised enough, Andy?

PAUL. Or shall we compromise even on our self-deception?
(ANDY *turns to them.*)

STONEY. My God, how old you look just now.

ANDY. How old we all look. We'll be very old soon, boys.

KATE. Andrew Cobham, when Brian Cambridge asked you to drop the five Golden Cities, what did you say?
(*Pause.*)

ANDY (*defiantly*). I said – aye.
(PAUL *walks to a part of the office where there are six rolled-up plans. He lays them on the desk, then he takes two and tears them in half.* STONEY *does the same with three others. All leave except* KATE. *After a long pause* ANDY *withdraws the last plan from the basket and unfolds it.*)

ANDY. It'll be a beautiful city. They'll own their houses, work in their factories and there'll be time for all that lovely living. It'll be a beautiful city. (*Exit.*)

KATE (*wearily*). It'll be a beautiful city.
Have you ever watched a city growing, ladies and gentlemen? Have you ever heard the hum of men building their golden city? The walls rise and the flowers blossom; the rubble turns to roads and the dust from machinery settles to reveal the slate and the granite, the glass and cement, and all the patterns men make for the pleasure of their living.
(MAITLAND *enters.*)

MAITLAND. … and all the patterns men make for the pleasure of their living. You all make lovely sounds when you talk about your city, lovely sounds. Why have you called me, Kate?

KATE. You know why.

MAITLAND. Are you snapping at me, Kate Ramsay? I know
it's favours and help you want but I've been friend to you
all for long enough now not to be resented.

KATE. You must speak to Andy again. Offer to bring industry
to the city.

MAITLAND. Have the unions turned down the resolution?

KATE. The unions, the unions! The unions would have to
empty half their coffers for such an enterprise.

MAITLAND. He won't bless you for urging this compromise.

KATE. Compromise? What compromise? That the workers
won't own the factory they work in? As if it makes much
difference whether they own the machine or not, they'll
still hate it. Do you really imagine I ever believed such
things would make a city golden? It'll be beautiful – enough!
There'll be no city like it in the world. They'll come
from the four corners – it'll be beautiful and that will be
enough.

MAITLAND. When will they decide?

KATE. Congress will vote in four months' time. Andy still
thinks they'll vote in favour after ten years – I know they
won't. His 'life-long' boys! He's become so obsinate he
can't find the strength to be honest.

MAITLAND. He won't listen to me, Kate; secretly he's always
been suspicious of a right-wing Minister like me being
around.

KATE. No, he's honest about you. He used to say, 'Old Maitland's earning a place in posterity, he wants to buy a piece
of heaven and God's good will, and the Golden City will
earn him a pass straight through the pearly gates.'

MAITLAND. Now he says?

KATE. 'Why shouldn't he buy his piece of heaven?' That's
what he says now. 'Let him buy his pass, I've tried to buy
mine.'

MAITLAND. I'll talk to him. After all, Kate, the city grows, the people in the city own their houses, the spirit of the place belongs to them and the co-ops have taken over most of the commerce. That's good, isn't it? He can't complain about that. Now he needs heavy industry, only my 'life-long' boys can provide that. Besides, he's got no alternative. But, you know, Kate, I can't do it alone; I can bring some money to the place but other people like Harrington will have to be involved.

KATE. Involve them.

> (JESSIE *appears carrying a tray of bottles of drink and some glasses.*)

MAITLAND (*to* KATE). I can't say I shall look forward to speaking to him. He'll snap. He snaps all the time. You all snap – been at it too long, Kate. All of you, a whole lifetime. He'll snap.

> (KATE *and* MAITLAND *leave.*
> JESSIE *picks up the plan of the Golden City and looks at it.*
> *She is older and weary. Everyone is older and weary.*
> *She takes a duster from her apron and slowly wipes down the desk, then she picks up the plan and looks at it again.*
> *We are in* ANDY'S *study.*)

ANDY (*off*). Nothing! I can find nothing in this house. A mess. it's all a great sprawling mess.

> (ANDY *enters. He wears a dressing-gown and he coughs.*)

JESSIE. Screaming? Still screaming, Andrew Cobham. Do you want to stay in your sick-bed longer?

ANDY. I can't have Maitland come here and see me in a dressing-gown – that jacket should have come back from the cleaners weeks ago, weeks.

JESSIE. Reggie Maitland is a Minister of Housing, he's a ruler, a man of power – he doesn't care. Now, sit in your chair, and I'll pour you a drink.

ANDY. You babble and fuss like an old washerwoman.

JESSIE. Do you want it neat or with soda?

ANDY. You *are* an old washerwoman.

JESSIE. I'll give you soda.

ANDY. And it's no good telling you. I tell you once, I tell you a dozen times, and still there's never a thing when I want it.

JESSIE. Heard from the office? How does the city grow?

ANDY. It grows.

JESSIE. What stage are you at?

ANDY. Stage? What would you know about building a stage?

JESSIE. You never talk, I have to squeeze words out of you. What stage are you at, I asked?

ANDY. Ten years have passed, it's two-thirds done – that stage.

JESSIE. Have all the people settled? They happy?

ANDY. Happy? Who knows? You can't leave misery behind, it comes with you. Ask their grandchildren.

JESSIE. And Paul and Stoney? Why do they stay away from here?

ANDY. They're tired. They work and they're tired. It's all routine now, they have private lives.

JESSIE. There was a time when your work kept you all together.

ANDY. You babble. You go on and on and you babble.

JESSIE. Friendship is a beautiful thing, you once said; people who share your – I'm sorry, I disturb you, don't I?

ANDY. Yes, you do.

JESSIE. I'm not much of a help to you, am I?

ANDY. Help? Help? You've mothered my children, you've kept my house, you cook, you mend – what other help can you give?

JESSIE. We don't even share walks to the smelly these days –

ANDY. Share, share! Everybody wants to share, everyone wants a bit of your peace or your love. Share? You share my bed.

JESSIE. You've no right, Andy, you've no right. I can't add to your work, all right, I can see this, you point these things out, you keep on and on pointing these things out, but you've no right to torment me.

'I'm a good mother, you say, I cook, I mend, I even iron your shirts to your satisfaction, but – words, I can never find words.

I'm not a fool; I've been made to feel it often enough, but I'm not a fool, even though I think you're right all the time, and – oh, if only I had the powers to argue and work it out – there's a wrong somewhere.

You said find your rightful place, I've found it. You said accept your limitations, I've accepted them – people should be happy with their limitations, you said. Happy! Me, happy! My only reward is to be treated like a hired housekeeper instead of your wife.

ANDY (*softer*). You babble, you babble, Jessie.

JESSIE. Don't you know what I'm saying? Don't you hear what I'm telling? I don't mind being inferior but I can't bear being made to feel inferior. I know I'm only a house-keeper but I can't bear being treated like one.

Wasn't it you wanted to treat everyone like an aristocrat? Well, what about me? I don't claim it as a wife, forget I'm your wife, but a human being. I claim it, as a human being. (*Pause.*) Claim? I'm too old to stake claims, aren't I? Like wanting to be beautiful, or enthusiastic or in love with yourself.

(*A pained, pained silence.*)

The city grows, you say?

ANDY. It grows.

JESSIE. And you're satisfied?

ANDY. Satisfied?

JESSIE. I shouldn't disturb you – rest.

(JESSIE *leaves*.

ANDY *sits alone a while. There is the sound of a doorbell, a door closes,* MAITLAND *enters.*)

MAITLAND. Andy, Andy – you're better then, good man, splendid. But you look morbid. You morbid?

ANDY. Morbid? I don't know. I just clench my teeth more, that's all.

MAITLAND. Holiday, take a holiday. I'll send you to a lovely spot I have in Greece. Go there, you don't know what pleasure it'd give me to offer you hospitality. Go there, Andy, go.

ANDY. I might, Reggie. I might at that.

MAITLAND. Excellent, excellent. Now then, I must be brief – I hate being brief, stupid life, never pausing for friendship; not even for a sickbed, stupid life. Still, let me explain. Kate's told me, the unions won't play, will they?

ANDY. There's not been a decision.

MAITLAND. I know, Andy, I know, but expectations, you must think ahead; what if they don't? They've turned it down nine times, what if they don't?

ANDY. There's not been a decision. Kate had no right. They're my boys, they're my lifelong boys and they won't let me down.

MAITLAND. Andy, Andy. I want to see that city finished, you know. I've helped it along and I want to see that city complete. I've got a proposition – I've come to offer help. Harrington can find one half of the industry you need – I can find the other. Don't scowl, man, I –

ANDY. Slow they are, slow and cautious – but sound. I've waited ten years and I can wait more –

MAITLAND. Oh, no, you can't, dear boy. Another year and you'll have unemployment on your hands, you know it, Andy, why be stubborn? We'll wait for Congress this year, of course we will. Do you think I wouldn't like to see the complete experiment work? I'm not a diehard, you

83

know this, but that city is beautiful, beautiful, we've nothing like it in the country – do you think I want to see it abandoned to ruin?

ANDY (*maudlin*). You see, Reggie, we've been at it for so long. I'd rather see it in ruins than make that compromise. Ruins don't matter, you can build on ruins, but future generations always want to look back and know that someone was around acting on principle. I want them to look back and know about me. I know you want it finished, you're a good man, but you mustn't ask me to make that compromise, not that one.

MAITLAND. But the architecture – future generations will want to look back at that too. That's a lifetime's work, that's a poet's work.

ANDY. I couldn't face myself, you see.

MAITLAND. Go to Greece. Go to the sun. You need the sun. Go to the sun and think about it.

ANDY. There's been no decision.

MAITLAND. We'll wait for it.

ANDY. When there's been a decision, I'll think about it.

MAITLAND. We'll wait for it, we'll wait.

(*In these last seconds, the light has been changing. MAITLAND leaves.*)

(*ANDY removes his dressing-gown to reveal a long white working-coat. The light grows and the scene becomes a magnificent abstract set of a building site and its scaffolding.*

ANDY stands and watches the scene change, listening to the howl of drilling, the whine of machines and the knock of hammers.

Till now, we've built an image of the Golden City through words – now, visually, for the first time we must see and feel the magic and excitement of a city growing.

As ANDY stands, he is joined by BRIAN CAMBRIDGE and TED WORTHINGTON.)

All three stand, watch and listen.)

CAMBRIDGE. It grows, lad, it grows.

ANDY. Aye, it grows.

WORTHINGTON. It's staggering what you've done, Andy, staggering.

ANDY. What's been decided?

WORTHINGTON. Not all you hoped for, Andy.

ANDY. What's been decided?

CAMBRIDGE. You didn't really expect them to vote in industry, you didn't really, did you? Private enterprise, let them do it, it's their job, not ours, Andy lad. Believe me, our own fights are enough. He didn't really hope for it, Ted.

ANDY. I hoped and I didn't hope – but?

CAMBRIDGE. But something happened.

WORTHINGTON. A last-minute amendment that suddenly ran like wildfire round all Congress.

CAMBRIDGE. True, like wildfire, great enthusiasm, round all the lads.

ANDY. It was?

CAMBRIDGE. To sponsor the last ten thousand inhabitants on your books.

WORTHINGTON. And more.

ANDY. More?

CAMBRIDGE. To erect a second trade-union centre in the Golden City.

WORTHINGTON. You've got another building to design, Andy.

CAMBRIDGE. You'd better get working again, hadn't you, lad?

WORTHINGTON. We want a fine building, the best of them all.

CAMBRIDGE. We'll fill it with paintings.

WORTHINGTON. And sculpture.

ANDY. And flowers.

CAMBRIDGE. Aye, and flowers.

(*Long pause. Then –*)

ANDY. Paul! Kate! Stoney!

85

CAMBRIDGE. What are you limping for, Andy?

WORTHINGTON. You hurt?

ANDY. My leg, didn't you know? I worked in the mines and one day the prop gave way and I used my leg instead, for five hours – till help came.

Paul! Kate! Stoney!

(ANDY *takes off the white coat to reveal an evening suit. His joviality is neurotic as his jubilation is pathetic.*

Now begins the preparation for the big banqueting scene. The table is being laid. The guests are arriving. The table is alight with candelabra.

ANDY *calls again for* KATE! STONEY! PAUL! *as before.*

There is no response.

He calls for a fourth time, like a man abandoned. Only KATE *appears. She is in evening dress.*

She takes her place at the table.

Soon everyone is seated.

The TOASTMASTER *knocks three times.*

Silence.

ANDY *faces them.*)

TOASTMASTER. My lords, ladies and gentlemen, pray be up-standing for your guest of honour.

(ANDY *walks slowly, with bows, to his place at the head of the table.*

Applause.

The guests sit.

The TOASTMASTER *again knocks three times.*)

My lords, ladies and gentlemen, pray silence for the Right Honourable Reginald Maitland, Her Majesty's Minister for Town and Country Planning.

(*Applause.*)

MAITLAND. My lords, ladies and gentlemen.

For those whose minds are mean, whose sense of national pride is bankrupt, it will be considered strange that a

86

Minister of the right should stand to pay tribute to a leader of the left. But a strong nation is not made by mean and bankrupt men; for this reason I have no hesitation in taking my place here tonight to extend, across the political barrier, a hand of sincere congratulations to one of our country's most brilliant architects. We all know his most famous and greatest achievement: for fifteen years I have watched and been proud to help, where I could, the building of the Golden City. The Labour movement can be proud of its son and those of us in the opposition who have had to work with him know – tough and resolute though he was – that he was a man who could keep his word, abide by agreements and not allow party politics to interfere with what we all knew to be right for the nation. And this nation, this proud little nation, knows, has always known how to honour and pay tribute to such men.

My lords, ladies and gentlemen, I give you – Sir Andrew Cobham.

ALL. Sir Andrew Cobham!

(SIR ANDREW *rises*.

Applause.)

ANDY. My lords, ladies and gentlemen. I am too old now to begin explaining and excusing the indulgences I allow myself. If the country where I was born and to whom I have given my best, sees fit to honour me, then I must allow it to honour me in the only way it knows how. Having spent a lifetime bullying traditionalists in order to bring into being a revolutionary project, it seems right to stop bullying for a moment and share at least one of the traditions of my opponents.

I suppose I will soon accustom myself to answering to the name, Sir Andrew – we accustom ourself to anything in old age. No, I mustn't be flippant, I'm honoured, and I'd be churlish and ungracious not to be – yes, churlish and ungracious not to be. After all, the Golden City is built; there were compromises but it's built, a hint, if nothing else, of what might be. It would be churlish and ungracious (*he coughs*), very churlish and foolishly ungracious –

ANDY *begins to cough violently.*

KATE *takes him by the arm and moves him to an armchair which* JESSIE *has pushed in for him.*

They remove his jacket and help him on with his dressing-gown.

In walking from the banqueting table to the armchair, ANDY *stoops and becomes older. He is older. It is many years later. It is* ANDY'*s study.*

Once he is seated in the chair, JESSIE *and* KATE *face each other from either side of it;* KATE *is holding his coat.* JESSIE'*s gaze challenges her right; finally* KATE *hands her the coat.*)

JESSIE (*to* KATE). You shouldn't have treated me like a hired housekeeper. You've damaged yourselves now, haven't you? Both of you, for all time.

(JESSIE *and* KATE *leave.*

ANDY *sits a long time alone, trying at times to rise, then slumping back, listlessly. Finally–*)

ANDY. I must stop clenching my teeth, I really must try and prevent my teeth from clenching. Howl, that's what I'd do if I opened my mouth – howl. Unclench your teeth, you old fool you. But why is it that I don't want to talk? Because I don't, you know, not a word. One day – I know it – one day I shan't even see people and then what'll happen. I shall stay just still like, petrified, because I won't be able to find a single reason why I should make one word follow another, one thought follow another.

There, look, my teeth were clenched again.

Do you know what depresses me? Men need leaders, that's what depresses me. They'll wait another twenty years and then another leader will come along and they'll build another city. That's all. Patchwork! Bits and pieces of patchwork. Six cities, twelve cities, what difference. Oases in the desert, that the sun dries up. Jake Latham, Jake Latham – ah, Jake Latham.

My lifelong boys! *My* lifelong boys? Prefects! That's all; the Labour movement provides prefects to guard other men's principles for living. Oh we negotiate for their better application, shorter working week and all that but – prefects! They need them, we supply them.

Still, nothing wrong in that I suppose; a bargain! A gentlemen's agreement, understood by everybody. They let us build the odd Golden City or two, even help us and in the end – look at me!

I don't suppose there's such a thing as democracy, really, only a democratic way of manipulating power. And equality? None of that either, only a gracious way of accepting inequality.

(JESSIE *enters, carrying a card table and a pack of cards.*

KATE, HARRINGTON *and* MAITLAND *also appear. They have come for a game of bridge.*)

Look again, they were clenched again. Unclench them. Silly old fool, you. Unclench them.

You shouldn't force people to dirty themselves. A man loves the world only when he loves himself, and what love do you have left for yourself, Andrew Cobham?

JESSIE. Talking to yourself again, Andrew Cobham. Yes, well, you always did, didn't you, old darling?

HARRINGTON. Has he been like this all evening, Jessie?

JESSIE. All evening and many evenings.

ANDY (*whispering*). They're good people, Jessie, all of them, you listen to me, good, good people.

(*They sit to play cards.*

JESSIE *sews.*

ANDY *deals.*)

ANDY. You know, Kate, a girl came up to me after a lecture one day and she said, 'Sir Andrew' – she spat out the 'Sir' – 'Sir Andrew,' she said, 'I don't believe you. You said all the things I believe in but I don't believe *you*.'

MAITLAND. Concentrate on the game, Andy, you're my partner now you know.

ANDY. We don't really like people, do we? We just like the idea of ourselves liking people.

KATE (*irritably*). Play, Andy.

ANDY. One heart.

HARRINGTON. Double.

MAITLAND. Re-double.

KATE. No bid.

ANDY. Three hearts.

HARRINGTON. No bid.

MAITLAND. Four hearts.

KATE. No bid.

> (HARRINGTON *plays a card.*
> MAITLAND *now lays down his cards.*)

ANDY. Thank you.

> (*The scene changes now to the cathedral.*
> *As the last characters slowly move away, young* ANDY *and* JESSIE *rush into the open space and from different directions. They look at each other and rush off again in new directions. Within seconds,* STONEY *rushes in from another direction, and off again.*
> *After another few seconds,* JESSIE *and* ANDY *slowly return from different parts of the cathedral. They have not found what they were looking for. They communicate their failure in silence and turn to* STONEY *who, in similar fashion, is also returning. Silence communicates failure also.*)

JESSIE. They've locked us in.

STONEY. Whose idea was it to explore the vaults? I knew we'd stayed there too long.

JESSIE. They've locked us in.

ANDY. I can't believe there's not one door open in this place.

JESSIE. You and your stories about golden cities – they've locked us in.

ANDY. I know there's a door open, I tell you.

(*Enter* PAUL.)

STONEY. Have you found one?

JESSIE. Is there – ?

(PAUL *keeps them in suspense*.)

PAUL. I've found one.

JESSIE. He's found one, he's found one – Paul's found an open door.

ANDY. Right, my ragged-arsed brothers – mount your horses.
(*Two of the boys link arms behind. The third grips their arms and bends down.* JESSIE *climbs on to his back and is now riding a 'chariot'.*)
We knew the door was open.

JESSIE. How did you know, my ragged-arsed brothers?

ANDY. Because we're on the side of the angels, lass.

JESSIE. – and are people good?

ANDY. Aye – and people are good.

JESSIE (*whipping them*). Giddy up, stallions. Forward, you ragged-arsed brothers – forward!
(*The 'chariot' gallops off.*
Moonlight strikes through the coloured glass.
Silence.)

END

NOTE

There is an alternative ending.

If one set of actors play both parts, then Old Andrew will have to be left on the stage after the bridge scene since it will be impossible for him to change back.

If two sets of actors play both young and old characters, then Old Andrew Cobham could still be left on stage after the bridge scene and the last cathedral scene could revolve round him as he says young Andy's lines – thus creating a dream-like effect; the 'flash-forward' will have become 'flash-back'. But in either case Old Andy must deliver Young Andy's lines wearily in contrast with the gaiety of the others, to retain the sad irony.